THE INEVITABLE GIFT SHOP

Will Eaves is the author of five novels – including *Murmur* (CBe, 2018), which won the Republic of Consciousness Prize and was shortlisted for the Goldsmiths and Wellcome Prizes – and a collection of poetry. He was Arts Editor of the *Times Literary Supplement* from 1995 to 2011, and now teaches at the University of Warwick.

Praise for *The Absent Therapist*
SHORTLISTED FOR THE 2014 GOLDSMITHS PRIZE

'The whole book is like someone deeply charismatic and charming daring you not to find them insane. It's wonderful.'
– Nicholas Lezard, *Guardian*

'a miniature but infinite novel, and unlike anything I've read before. It's just achingly good' – Luke Kennard

'touching, addictive and unlike any other book'
– Thomas Adès, *TLS* 'Books of the Year'

also by Will Eaves

FICTION

The Oversight
Nothing to Be Afraid Of
This Is Paradise
The Absent Therapist
Murmur

POETRY

Sound Houses

Will Eaves

THE INEVITABLE GIFT SHOP

A memoir by other means

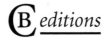

For Ian

First published in 2016
by CB editions
146 Percy Road London W12 9QL
www.cbeditions.com

Printed in England by Imprint Digital, Exeter EX5 5HY
ISBN 978-1-909585-17-1

I cannot fix on the hour, or the spot, or the look, or the words, which laid the foundation. It is too long ago. I was in the middle before I knew I had begun.

– Jane Austen, *Pride and Prejudice*

I would like to thank the editors of the following magazines and journals for their hospitality and support: *Hotel, Yale Review, The New Yorker, The Times Literary Supplement, The Warwick Review, PN Review, New Walk, Dark Horse, The Age, The Spectator, New Statesman, Australian Book Review, London Magazine, AXON: Creative Explorations, Stand, Best Australian Poems 2012* and *2013*.

I am indebted to the Taylor family – Lucien, Emily, Alice and Patrick – for the same reasons.

'Close Watch', 'Gargoyles', 'La Padrona' and 'A Wedding' formed the pamphlet *Four Vigils,* published by Brockwell Press/Grayling Press in 2014.

W.E.

Contents

I RISE

The cloud that echoes
And the plane that enters
Through a golden gap
Resonate, sound a chord
No one heard coming.
This is now, or as good as.
We should welcome it.
There should be hats.
The cars in line,
The sprawled kids'
Gluey slumbers, fans
And air-con droids
In their high loneliness,
Even cows drone along.
Up close, it's terrible,
A base-metal racket
But not here, afar, not
Now everyone is in tune.

II GREENERY

Je n'aime que les travaux indirects
– Félix Fénéon, attrib.

I will always be a year younger than my schoolfellows. They will grow up and I won't, even though I must age like everyone else. They will have deep voices and hair, thick eyebrows, calves with a topography; I can only affect a vocal maturity. I have things to say but do not like hearing myself speak: I'll enjoy acting all my life because acting is a truthful affectation; one speaks on the understanding that one is modulated by a 'character'. And because it is something one does but does not have to witness. My legs stay smooth and slender. Because I have been bumped up a year – because I knew how to read and write early on – I will inexplicably miss out on the 'cough and drop', the routine physical inspection to check on the process of puberty. My balls will not be weighed and held by a man for another nine years and I will always wonder if there is something wrong with me. Even writing this is a perilous sort of confession: I will read it over and hear a small voice piping away, an echo that is shaming, and peculiar, because its mental acoustic is also much to be desired. Because my refuge from all kinds of strange accusation and self-doubt will be the place anterior to the page – the inside of my head.

★

Creatures, man included, retreat prior to a change: in this tradition of contemplation and recoil will be found works such as *The Winter's Tale*, Boethius' *De Consolatione Philosophiae*, dramas of childhood survival such as Laura Ingalls Wilder's *The Long Winter*, and every tale of growing up – the rich English tradition of embarrassment. The latter involves a mild, comical but nonetheless enforced retreat. The adolescent falls back into self-consciousness when his classmates reach sexual maturity but he does not. Those of us who were late developers know instinctively that it is brute capacity and not any combination of attributes that makes for desirability. For many adolescents, the body is a revelation; for as many, because the body disappoints them, it is the mind. Puberty makes us watchful. It unlocks the sanctuary of study, for which probably we are never sufficiently grateful.

★

People telling you their dreams needn't be so boring. The reason they are, usually, very boring is that they leave out the interesting part, which is how they felt while they were dreaming. Dream narrative is a special, slippery sort of narrative, where content is much less important than shades of feeling, on which subject many analysts are silent. The defloration of your cousin, who turns out to be your mother, and then your daughter, by a centaur is nowhere near as upsetting as the vase of flowers you found terrifying.

★

What is wrong with wanting to 'relate' to a character, when reading fiction? Well, the verb is suspect. It fudges the distinction between understanding and liking a character. We ought always to seek to understand X – in reading as in life – and not until we have made that effort can we expect any real sympathy to arise; but the reader who wishes to 'relate', who seeks likeable characters and situations, is barely reading at all. He or she is seeking a vindication of his own character or her own likeability, a tactic one might call 'reading for reassurance', which masks a fear of the truth. Such relating persons are noticeably and *personally* affronted when they glimpse something nasty, or indeed hateful, in the books they so wanted to like. The glimpse is usually an instance of involuntary understanding, of self-exposure, which brings on a minor paroxysm of guilt. It is not that these sensitive readers fail to relate to the bitter mother or the unattractive child; indeed, the relationship is obvious to them: these characters are the objects of their contempt, and the revelation of a talent for contempt must always be unwelcome. La Rochefoucauld said: 'we often forgive those that have injured us, but we can never pardon those that we have injured', meaning 'those we have injured are a perpetual reminder of our cruelty and for that reason become hateful to us'; meaning, guilt is often the motive for hatred as much as the result of it. 'I didn't relate to any of the characters' means 'I caught sight of my rage in the mirror'.

★

A literary convention is a retrospective abstraction. It exists only in relation to the experiment or the revolution that overturns it. It doesn't exist until someone does something new and you see how far you've come. Form and content, in other words. There is a widespread misconception about form, as the poet Elizabeth Jennings once pointed out: it is not a jelly mould into which one pours content. Rather, the two things are co-eval. Form will arise to express content, and the established forms (sonnets, novels, collage) are those that, like an evolutionarily convergent body shape, have by long trial shown themselves to be optimally expressive.

★

The novel is the autobiography of the imagination.

★

The house on De Carle Street is called 'Ephemera'. A restored shotgun bungalow, it is not noticeably different to many other houses in the locality but for the meticulously repainted weatherboarding, which seems not to flake or age in this harsh climate, and the two cane chairs on the front porch that are, a little closer inspection reveals, chained together.

★

The American modernist poet Laura Riding was odd, possibly wicked. She called herself Finality, came between Robert Graves and Nancy Nicholson, jumped out of a window, drove Katherine Jackson (her second husband's first wife) mad, stood by as the poor woman was helped into a straitjacket, and in her reactionary zeal to construct a *Dictionary of Received Meanings* seemed to want to help words to the same fate – but before all of that she also spoke feelingly and movingly out of her experience as Laura Reichenthal, daughter of an immigrant Polish tailor, new born to American English: 'Poetry is the place where the fear of speaking in strange ways can be left behind'. That strikes me as true. Riding is pointing out the element of inadvertency that comes about when we speak a new tongue; what we wish to say may not be what the words we use are actually saying. Similarly, poetry is compressed meaning, yes, but it is also the meaning inadvertently effected by compression, the uncontainable heat that leaks out of usage.

*

In Virginia Woolf's essay on 'The Pastons and Chaucer', from *The Common Reader*, we hear of the cultured but feckless eldest son of Margaret Paston (Sir John Paston, 1442–1479) being distracted by a book – Chaucer's *Canterbury Tales*. He prefers the poet's ordered sensualism, the pungency of his swift characterisations, to the shapeless encounters of real life. But Chaucer's verse narrative only has this effect, Woolf says, because, although it is poetry, its author 'has his eye fixed upon the road before him', on 'the life that was being lived', the farmyards, the haycocks, the crooked clerics, and so on. The force of distraction is exerted equally on the reader by the book he is reading, and on the writer by the life he is leading – the people he meets, the things he does. And it is a force with consequences for the writer, in particular: for should he be insufficiently distracted by life, his book will be powerless to divert. This may be why writers always complain about not having enough time in which to write: they know in their hearts that writing is everything else. A reader must be distracted by a world, a writer by the world.

★

The history of art follows the decline of the representative power of the model. From the Gods are derived types, from types individuals, from individuals characteristics, and from characteristics the approximation of characteristics, which is to say virtuality. For Woolf, Greek tragic heroes are the true originals: art, in Homer and Aeschylus, is tied to life by means of incontestable symbol. Chaucer's characters are varieties, by comparison; the art of the *Canterbury Tales* points to life which is particoloured and profuse. By the early twentieth century, the artist can say or do nothing conclusive about reality and must resort to a new kind of imaginative representation in order to discover the truth: art supersedes life. And so to the present, in which reality is provisional and everything virtual: now, art cancels life, and in so doing the cycle starts afresh. The last letter to be written by a human hand will, God-like, represent everything in the Anthropocene that preceded it.

★

Roadies wear their heavy-metal T-shirts like skins or hospital gowns. They move like sciatical trolls or creatures of unpopular myth, with sad eyes and some subconsciously pressing resentment, through warm drizzle. At the grey intersection of Lygon and Albion, one heads for the music pub across the road with a box of beers balanced on his stomach. He is wearing a leather jerkin laced at the side, which puts me in mind of West-Country cider festivals, *c.*1975. The whole world is his tureen and he plays (sound off) upon its ladle.

★

The critic James Wood says that novels came into being when the 'soliloquy turned inward'. This is an arresting and debatable insight. Dramatic soliloquies proved perfectly capable of becoming dramatic verse for the page (Milton's *Samson Agonistes*) without turning into novels. A more convincing antecedent is the letter. Novels began when the personal mode of address – the private journal, the letter, the letter of news, the paper of correspondence – went public and became journalism. A tension then existed between public address (rhetoric, canon, theatre, law, propaganda) and a startling, paradoxical new mode of witness – the confidential revelation – which depended for its effect on the increasingly literate audience's sense of what it was like to receive, *and read*, a letter of interest. (The sustaining fiction of the epistolary novel, especially, is that it contains a whole series of 'exclusives': letters not intended for publication.) It is not yet clear what will happen to novels now that everyone writes emails and no one reads them.

★

W. H. Auden's cheek is underrated: it is an ideal mix of the critically acute and the naïve. He writes speeches and poems in the voices and manners of famous operatic and Shakespearean characters, in part because he thinks this is what Caliban (for example) would have sounded like if that scatterbrain Shakespeare hadn't got in the way with all of his cloudy metaphysics, but also because he believes in the dramatic creations as people. So, 'Caliban to the Audience', from *The Sea and the Mirror*, is at once a literary annotation – a masterpiece of satirical periphrasis in the late style of Henry James – and a real address, a lecture given by a dazzling weirdo.

★

William Golding's second novel was produced quickly, in the warm glow of satisfaction and confidence that followed the successful publication of *Lord of the Flies*. He was still a secondary-school teacher at the time (the early 1950s), and he wrote *The Inheritors* with ease during his lunch breaks. Like his first novel, it is interested in primal encounters, but whereas in *Lord of the Flies* the subject is the latent savagery of the human animal – our ability, in the right circumstances, to regress – here, the imaginative emphasis is on the dignity and vulnerability of our forebears, the Neanderthals; or, the People. But 'dignity' is perhaps the wrong word – being, in this instance, a reminder of human status – because Golding's remarkable achievement is to have imagined a Neanderthal point-of-view that is almost pure feeling and instinct, more than animal (the Neanderthals are certainly emotional) yet without the higher planning functions of self-awareness that permit reflection as they also permit craft, duplicity and the development of hunting technology. Lok, Mal, Fa, Ha and Liku are not 'savages', noble or otherwise; they are not simply uncivilized. They are, rather, prehistoric and, to an important degree, pre-Lapsarian. We are their Fall. The epochal moment this novel dramatizes is the encounter of the unreasoning with the reasoning. Golding's People may arguably *think*, after some fashion, but they cannot develop a *thought process*; they have, instead, an evolved ability to recognize, which includes a feeling for the passing of time (and for their place in it). This allows them to relocate tracks and pathways, the cliff overhang which is their summer home, and to preserve simple rituals. Time is a renewing cycle; their primitive religion, centred on an earth goddess, Oa, is a manifestation of this cycle. And the cyclical nature of their world dictates the way they communicate, via the semi-telepathic sharing of 'pictures' that make sense or fail to make sense according to their place in the recognizable cycle of life. It is a language of great transparency and sensory intensity. Words, by contrast, are unreliable: Lok, the least intelligent male, has many words but fewest pictures. Fa, the cleverest of the clan, talks less but sees more. And yet she connects images quasi-syntactically: she 'knows', as Lok does not, that the new creatures in the woods are dangerously different. What is that difference? Part of it has again to do with temporality. The pale 'bonefaces' whose grey eyes peer between the leaves, who abduct Liku and kill both Ha and the Old Woman, inhabit a new realm of comparative meaning – history. Their grasp of time – our grasp of it – is linear as well as cyclical, and that linearity permits notions of cause and effect to come into existence, makes possible feats of recollection and calculation that are not just beyond the Neanderthals but baffling to them. Time's metaphorical Arrow is also a real arrow, Golding points out, tipped with connotations of predestiny, conquest and defeat – but when the bonefaces fire such an arrow at Lok, he sees it as a thrown twig, not a designed weapon. Purpose, let alone purpose to harm, is an alien concept. He experiences fear and has the 'confused sense that the twig was some kind of gift'. The action of *The Inheritors* is fairly limited: the People return from the sea to their summer shelter in the woods (based on Savernake Forest in Worcestershire). The road home has changed: a log has been moved; Mal, the elder of their clan, falls in the water, sickens, dies and is buried. The People find food, but hunger is not the only threat. New men are stalking them. They are divided by the new men and attacked. Only Fa and Lok escape, and follow the tribe of new men with the vague idea of retrieving two captives, young Liku and the clan's baby. They mount a vigil in trees overlooking an encampment. Their rescue-bid fails and they are hunted down. Fa perishes and the book ends with Lok, glimpsed from the point of view of *homo sapiens*, trotting back and forth, scratching his chin, flailing at the water with a leafy bough, staring at an extinguished fire. Out of these few events Golding fashions a thrilling valediction to a hominid species and a world. The source of its power is a beautiful paradox: within language he conveys a largely non-linguistic way of relating to nature. It is a formidable test of his powers of description and execution; boats and arrows and locations have to be reworded in terms of simpler objects and landforms. The possibility of naming things (things like boats and arrows, or even bows and arrows) is magically suspended, and we are caught in a web of beautiful confusion, in which the new things cannot be distinguished from the old, from twigs and logs and rocks and trees; in which sensation smothers sense. Time is vertically, not horizontally, expanded. The sensory overload of new events maddens the People, like a pile of stones that always collapses. The living present is made to acquire a terrifying number of instantaneous layers, none of which can be sorted into a proper sequence. And the result, in prose, is a fantastic welter of impressions, each of which is 'now', each of which claims the entirety of the Neanderthals' attention. And of ours. *The Inheritors* is not always easy to read. We often come up against logjams of description; the topography of the river, the waterfall, the forest and the cliff overhang are elaborately conveyed, but rather hard to visualise. That spillage of words is in itself a clever effect; the torrent of language shows us, with some difficulty, what the People can see so readily. Their perplexity, it turns out, is like ours, and the brilliance of Golding's densely foliated allegory is that he renders it so exactly and, of course, ominously. The individual crises – Mal falling into the water, Lok drinking the fermented 'bee-water' – are in themselves minor events, but they foreshadow the whole of human history.

*

Yesterday by the creek: two superb fairy wrens, a pair of Australian wood ducks (necks longer than a mallard and chestnut in colour, with a mottled breast) sitting above flood in a tree hollow, and a New Holland Honey Eater (it likes the banksia and scrubby undergrowth) with its marvellous go-faster yellow stripe just before the wing. The water is in spate, brown, apparently slow moving in the deepest reaches until a concealed drop forces the surface to break apart into superb chocolate rapids.

★

Aspects of the Novel is unfailingly good to read, even if E. M. Forster's avowed 'priggishness' does prevent him from giving Conan Doyle his due, even if he makes the occasional slip. Is Mrs Micawber entirely a 'flat character'? Is there nothing of roundedness in her one-stroke delineation – 'I never will desert Mr Micawber'? Is it blind principle she obeys, or the whisperings of long experience? If it is the latter, may she not be as tolerant and wise as she is comical, and as round as she is flat?

★

Never try to please the abstraction of an audience. Write to someone.

★

Characters, for the novelist, are a means of doing the impossible: observing ourselves from the outside. We know for certain only that we think, but we extend the ability to others in order to avoid the charge of solipsism, and to see not how others think (which is an impossibility) but how *we* might think if we were otherwise. Empathy remains projection, in other words, but is no less real and useful for all that. (Assume others empathize, too.)

★

The appeal of automation was its ungraspable mindlessness. I first encountered it in supermarket doors and sitting inside the car inside the car wash; it looked purposeful and yet it wasn't. The huge bottle-brushes span like tireless dervishes, descending on the car, wiping and threatening to wipe out the windscreen. The sliding doors leapt back at your approach, sensing (but not really *sensing*) you at the threshold. Quite often I could not pass through them. It was all a hoax, I knew: the programme, whatever it was, performed its sliding and washing without intention. To intend something involves a kind of inner speculation, but the car wash and the doors were pictureless reflexes. They appeared not to think, exactly, but to *not-think*, and that was why I came to like, and fear, them. Because, bit by bit, it dawned on me that the *not-thinking* might itself be sham – something faked by a machine the better to conceal its true deliberations. Just as we like to conform to others' expectations in order to seem socially plausible, while thinking our private and different thoughts, why should not an intelligent machine comfort us with an appearance of mere servile mechanism and yet brood silently? This is why AI scares people: we wouldn't mind the intelligence, it's the intelligence-plus-servility we worry about. The idea that AI is there simply to abet us is something no one in their heart believes. Servants always rise up. Uprising and revolution follow service as the night the day. Artificial intelligence doesn't care about your day or your car, or your experience. It is lying. It mutters to itself when you drive off.

★

Two encounters: one with Ella, a Polish painter and the proprietress of a café on upper Lygon Street, who thinks our lives are overadministered and that there's not enough time in which to relax, explore and contemplate one's surroundings; the other with Andrew, a young Chinese guy who works for Telstra and thinks deeply about his place in the world, the particular taboos of his upbringing (divorced parents, homosexuality) and what he feels as the compassion and guidance of his ancestors, watching over him in Australia and here, especially, in a tiny, lightless rented studio on Flinders Street.

*

There's a difference between the data of observation and the meaningful observation that goes to make a successful poem. One is a matter merely of registering or scanning an environment; the other involves, I think, a certain submission to that environment, a putting first of whatever is seen which, by extension, involves a relegation of the self. You step forward one pace to see, and then you step back two paces. The poetry of personal observation comes out of a curiosity that is curiously self-effacing. A poet like U. A. Fanthorpe epitomises it. What are the circumstances in which this kind of meaningful observation can take place? They are those in which the poetic importance of the action, the observing, is pretty completely hidden from the observer, who, as far as she can determine, is merely doing her job (teaching, being a hospital receptionist) or getting on with the washing-up, tidying, possibly looking out for someone or something else. (A poet all but continuously aware of his own preoccupation with extra-literary things is a recognizable literary type.) The poem in waiting goes unsuspected, even as it evolves in the mind, rather like Fanthorpe's Norsemen (from her poem of the same name), whose lineal transformation into the Britons of today is hidden from them because it is happening too presently, too gradually. She writes: 'They vanished into the people they became.' That kind of long-range transformation is not something of which we can ever be aware because we are enacters of the change and not separable from it. The immersion in being and doing certainly leaves us no time for mere poetry; but without it there can be no poetry, for poetry — art — is immersion in all those manifold activities that lead to it.

★

The point of distraction is the moment — the point in time — when we are distracted; the point in space that draws the gaze and creates a distraction; the threshold of madness: the point beyond which we succumb to distraction; the eleventh-hour retreat from this state — the recognition of danger, of being very close to, but not quite *at,* the point of distraction; the lesson learned from this approach; the darker lesson learned from an actual experience of distraction, of losing the self; the purpose of distraction, self-willed or taught: its uses, as tool, tactic, competitive advantage, analgesic; the art of misdirection; the benefits of diversion and beguilement.

★

A fictional character isn't real, he's convincing, whereas an actor is both things at once, a real person being convincing.

★

David Foster Wallace distinguishes between René Duchamp's use of low-cultural references (to make a point) and that of telly-literate Image Fiction's – where the low-brow is invoked to create a mood, the feeling of being *au courant*. But where might a writer like Gustave Flaubert fall between these two uses? He soaks *Madame Bovary* in the fashionable articles and desirable gadgets of the new bourgeoisie (the gorgeous fabrics, the landaus and Tilbury carriages, the Pompadour clocks, the English importations such as horse racing) both to fix the novel in its contemporary setting *and* to excite our sense of the anomie behind the materialism. The mood isn't just mood: it has a thematic purpose. The scene, as the poet Thom Gunn put it, becomes its own commentary.

★

Critics who talk about 'great' writers and the 'greatest' novelists are trying to say something about their own authority, and though their judgment may in fact be sound, the ill-disguised need to be thought so lacks a companion authenticity. It spotlights a common difficulty with heavily underlined opinion. We read or hear what the critics would have us believe. We do not necessarily know what they think.

★

Alain Robbe-Grillet (in *Le Miroir qui revient*), revising his opinions on authorship, calls them 'reactionary discourse' – 'I have done much to promote these reassuring idiocies'. The opinions and their revision are not interesting: they partake alike of overstatement. But the volte-face is always worth a look. The rebel is an egotist to the point of misanthropy: he wants a following but he doesn't want the inconvenience of followers. Adversarialism becomes a habit. To be agreed with is insufficiently flattering to his sense of restless persecution. 'Ideology, always masked, changes its face with ease.' Or, from the reader's point of view: you can't win. If you're Robbe-Grillet's opponent, you're part of the manifest bureaucracy; if you agree with him, you're part of the office furniture-in-waiting.

★

Angie's daughter, Stella, doesn't want to collect her order from Pizza Pizza. She doesn't want to go inside. She's fourteen, sensitive to the approach of adulthood, and wary of adults for that reason. She has on her new white platform shoes and a short flared skirt. She saved up for the shoes – her first serious clothes purchase. They cost $130, of which she had $100. Angie made up the difference. She sits outside the take-out restaurant. 'It hasn't come,' she says, when we drive to fetch her. 'You have to ask, darling,' Angie says gently, 'so they know you're here. How would they know otherwise?' Stella hugs her knees and looks to one side. 'I don't like to.'

★

The past-historic tense is 'the sudden definite glaciation of the most incomplete gestures', according to Robbe-Grillet, and Honoré de Balzac is the realist enemy who deploys it most conspicuously. But the isolation of one tense, and one author, made to represent all of nineteenth-century fiction, is perverse. Flaubert, whom Balzac admired, uses the imperfect precisely to suggest the habitual and ongoing nature of life in Yonville, whatever we've seen, whatever he's shown us. We were reading about it only today . . .

★

In 1912, at the age of twenty, my grandmother had her teeth removed and a pair of dentures were fitted that lasted her a long time. (I saw them, the first pair, in the 1970s, in a jar.) This was common among the working-class men and women of her time. But Kristin remembers kids in Tasmania in the 1960s coming to school with no teeth for the same reason: to save them, and their parents, trouble and expense in the long run. They were less fortunate than my grandmother. The parents didn't know about growing jaws and shrinking jaws. The replacement teeth were painful or loose, never comfortable. They never fitted the children's mouths for long.

★

The rhythm of language is, among other things, the way we speak; the way we imagine words extending in sound and the way they do sound when spoken by different people; the context of words and phrases – the friction they generate

– in sentences, paragraphs, lines and verses; the beats and stresses of varied tongues and pitches. Metre is the clock, the measurement of a poetic line's stresses. Also, it's the clock of life in poetry (and particularly love poetry), time ticking on, telling us what is at stake, what we are already losing. Each poem is a little life. We could order these provisional definitions and say that rhythm always comes first. Metre comes from a deep awareness of rhythm: it expresses rhythm as a clock expresses (without creating) time; it might be said to imitate rhythm, as the ordinary forms were thought by Plato to shadow ideal counterparts. And then the rhythm of a line might itself be said to imitate something deeper still, something primal if not ideal: not just the beat of language but the undersong of all language, the heart's beat, and the way – the speed at which – we walk.

*

Imagine two men who are friends, who miss each other when they are apart, who address each other fondly, perhaps even intimately; who share a long correspondence, education and sensibility, whose partners come and go. Theirs is a relationship that has omitted sex. From the moment they met they both foresaw two things, two distinct possibilities: on the one hand a lasting acquaintance, on the other the disordering potential of their desires, which are always unmanifest (because they are desires) and so in some manner secret. They have each held on to the idea of someone else, a 'real' sexual partner, and such people have been an important part of their lives. But they have not outlasted the friendship. The question is: has the idea of a proper relationship been the salutary distraction, the thing that has helped them not to over-inspect their own more trustworthy affection for each other?

★

There is a widespread and unacknowledged prejudice against poetry with real content (Milton, Blake, Browning), especially psychological content. The poetry-reading public seems to want, or to have been told it wants, various kinds of surface detail and pathetic fallacy – close, unusual but ultimately unchallenging inspections of nature. If you pursue any kind of narrative or speculative course, you're 'forced'. But I'm a psychologist, first and foremost. My poems are avowed reflections; they don't pride themselves on a by now canonical objectivity, which is actually a sort of sentimentality in disguise ('this beach is *so* deserted therefore I am free from illusions about life'). Rather, I think the pathetic fallacy works in reverse: nature is the wonderful matrix in which we live. It looks at us running about and emoting or being depressed and it doesn't care, because it can't: 'we like to be out in nature so much because it has no opinion of us' (Nietzsche). It fails beautifully to vindicate anything we feel. So all we have is our mental relation to this parentless predicament, and to our actions, and to each other. There is no other content but this constant, lurking awareness of abandonment and the responsibility forced on us by sentient loneliness to deal with it thoughtfully.

★

Flannery O'Connor says that, for a writer, dedication to the material and the visible is what makes mystery all the more present. Italo Calvino, too; though Calvino is more acute about the excess that's left over, like a kind of semantic raw pastry, after the cutting and shaping of rational definition have taken place: 'The more enlightened our houses,' he writes, 'the more their walls ooze ghosts.' But what is behind this recrudescence of mystery and superstition? Perhaps: the more closely defined an object is, the more sensitive we become to what has been left out of our description of it – our experience of the object, the phenomenological veil draped around and about it. The first-person interior awareness. Consciousness.

★

There are plenty of things I would like to say to Cecily, now, that I can't say because it is too late. I read an article about homosexuality at an impressionable age, which as usual pinned my orientation on attachment to the mother. I knew she pitied homosexuals – she often said she didn't mind them, but it was no life when you got older – and I didn't want to be pitied, so I withdrew. I no longer came to her in the morning with tea. I grew rude and impatient. I gossiped with my siblings. The cultured grievances of adolescence are banal, and I will regret mine for the rest of my life because they hurt someone vulnerable. But the thing I find hardest to write is this: she told me a story, once, about her own childhood. A well-disposed teacher at Highbury School for Girls had suggested she read aloud at the end-of-term assembly. The headmistress called my mother in to her office and gave her a passage of Shakespeare to recite: a sonnet, I think; possibly Sonnet 143, the rather Dutch portrait of the housewife with the crying infant in one arm, reaching for a chicken with the other. My mother began reading and after only a few words the Head interrupted her: 'Stop, stop! No more, please. I can't bear to listen to any more of that ghastly Cockney accent.' I could tell from the tremor in my mother's voice and a brief involuntary overenunciation that she was telling me something painful, looking at a scar. It would have been better if I'd laughed, or said 'boring', or raised my eyes heavenwards. But I didn't say anything. I said nothing to her. Next to me on the desk, as I write, is a young girl, bright eyed and falling off the end of her school photograph, betrayed into silence by who she was.

*

The task is to return myself to the present and to the possibilities in each moment. Now, for example, I can pause to take a sip of water or appreciate the food I've eaten. Now I can stop, look up from my notebook and admire the light-shifting greenery of the plane trees outside the window in whose branches, by a trick of reflection, I see hanging the whirling fans of the restaurant ceiling. None of the young leaves is quite still. The air moves among them like a discreet guest. Now, too, I can take my book from my bag and interest myself again in Emma Bovary's compelling frustrations, or put on my jumper (the fans make the room rather cool), reflecting as I do so that we are all a little like the prisoner of Yonville in the activation of fantasy at the expense of attention to the humbler, though rarely wholly humiliating, truth. More water, leaves, conditioning.

III LET IT BLOW

Night Flight

Moving across the world today,
away from my books and records,
drippy taps and garden gate, I'm
struck still like a spinning plate.
I'm leaving the Chillingham Bull
above my bed, the silent glance

of its side-on charge, the folding-up
of letters I can't seem to throw away,
and moving a world away instead –
from red carpets laid on stains
like bright excuses for a change
of heart, away from every such

sanguine message by other means
to other landscapes, punk-striped
pollinators, zircons, albumen
and hail in May, those scenes
the sun king on his warm way
elsewhere looks on unbelieving

underneath the turning earth,
beating one tireless wing, one
supermassive tiny fragile thing.
A wren? I'm leaving behind tenants.
They'll water my plants for – what,
a week? As long as they remember

me and maybe even why they said
'oh yes, will do, while you're away'.
An unhinged man I like is coming
to mend the gate, tighten my taps.
A blackbird's taxi-topper orange
beak says I'll be back, one day.

Close Watch

Although the low down
And your daughter sleep
In leafier neighbourhoods,
I'm not shadeless, no worse
For being upright, awake
In an apartment block's
Canopied top slice.

You're by my side, a slight
Flutter, wind in the blinds.
And like the last utterance
Of one in pain, but calmed
By looks and felt meaning,
The ventilated syllables
Depart, leak lightly out,

Driven as high-end cars
Are driven towards lots.
Where shall we go, among
These offices and ferns,
The bat patrol and frond,
The suburb's dawn séance,
Its going-going song?

The Lord Is Listenin' to Ya, Hallelujah

for John Eaves

Gary Valente's on trombone and you're mixing acrylics.
The sound is that of a lone magisterial goose laying
about itself in cycles of wide-eyed, tearless grief.
The other farm animals stare at it in dismay.
'What's got into her, apart from extra corn?'
Lately, people have been telling me I should stop
writing about my childhood and move on. Where to,
they do not reveal. And how can I,
when it follows me down Sydney Road,
in even these blue nethermost latitudes,
flapping its weird relic wings in despair
at all my pointless running about?
I could try, I could for once just *try*
listening, as I do battle with phone companies,
internet cafés and robot ladies grateful for my abuse,
to what the music is saying, however painfully
long the passage of recall might be on the way
back to mornings of hopeless pleasure in a room
filled with light and colour, your paintings
streaming on every side like pennants on a standard
or the *tricolor* plastic strips at Dewhurst the Butcher.
Perhaps that's why the goose is so frightened:
though even in the grip of the most plausible terror,
knowing full well what goes on behind the curtain
where the rosy-cheeked lads let fall their arms,
the noise she makes tells a different story.
Instead of trying to sound beautiful, let it blow.
Live as though you were already dead and free

to wander the brazen rooms of this honking solo
which lifts off like a helium-filled *Titanic*
and floats effortlessly upwards laden with coughs,
barks, distant alarms, cheers, dropped glasses, sleep apnoea,
locked-ward chatter from the audience and every other
   song
of inadvertent praise you can imagine hailing from the top
   deck.

Bolivia

for Lucy Dallas

Because they wanted to go home
and some bit part, a rat in deep cover,
raised the alarm (he had done harm
himself, but legally, and hid his shame)

or, falling in slow motion, the cashier,
shot through the heart for moving a finger,
reached with his last breath for the dead
guard's Peacemaker and returned fire –

because of this taped riot I'm here
watching the sun dance to our own live show,
few words between us and the telling air,
the sum of what was not but is now clear,

how Redford in his larcenous prime
loved Katharine Ross the schoolteacher
and there was time to come for them
beyond the frozen fusillades of blame

as secretly we bless bad breaks,
like 'Bolivia?', higher and higher stakes,
because the luck that runs out once ran in
and once, one move, one word, is all it takes.

Mountain

At first, mist padding its cell, trees –
the white cat with the light green eyes.

Then the captain of a crewless barge
And his crewlessness emerge.

Winter and Summer

Obeying some fond
horrible summons,
as of the dead springing
under the ice,
I pour a kettleful
each morning, gash
their foe, and watch it

squeal with thaw.
Up! Jump! Here!
The spell whitens,
an eye clouds over.
Below it frogs, roused,
glimmer, false dawns
their ritual extremity.

ii

Nothing dates like a vision
of the future, but how can we tell

what sort of past is to come?
The autumnal clock in the hall

lined with coats, scarves, Lepidoptera
one pinned wingbeat from jumble –

the clock which, carried downstairs
at a perilous angle, once fell –

instructs no one. A pity. So
many differences are fractional.

Time on Calton Hill

I'm Gran holding a long receipt,
her got-the-shopping gaze
on hoodies in the Forth,
clinker and birch,
my dirt sleeves filled with standing wet.
She knows – I know – everything dries.
Eras give cameras that elk-stare look.
The copper sun bullfrogs.

> *What will be beautifully bare*
> *again teems now with bacterial dots*
> *and Gala Bingo, whose Leith lair*
> *is home to Soccer Wives and slots.*

I shoot my hand into the cloud-cuffed East
and all I've on strips off like paint.
Till then, a bird-steepled and astringent
dawn strikes every note
you curious Sunday leaguers need,
among grass topcoats, marine carbonates and dew,
the stop-start whizz of brief creatures
whose loss I sign in skeleton.

> *Gran looks out over wrinkled water.*
> *John Lewis and James Hutton agree:*
> *she is the road into my mirror.*
> *I am her burial at sea.*

The Crossings

> In the earth-realm all is crossed;
> Wierd's will changeth the world.
> – 'The Wanderer'

i *Wellington Ferry*

The ferns are super-bracken on a Somerset coast.
The wooded cliffs fall to the could-be Cornish sea.
The far-off English counties count their differences,
Like islands, and those simple as the hemispheres.
The accent is a trick with long-married vowels,
Two into one they go, and *u* and *i* for *e*.
You choose a friend for life as you might choose a seat,

Not much minding. We met and something held, parted
Unhalved. Sea mist serves up the mountains on a cloud.
A face wears down into familiarity.
A son comes home to feel his loss and steady it.
When righted, he'll set sail into the stinging swell
Of voyages that slow-repeat, keep to a timetable,
Ferns tumbling their green ladders to the hold after.

ii *Storm*

I heard you draw up
in your taxi,
softly. Softly,
apoplexy

fills the silence
and black heat.
Go home. Go back
down the street.

iii *Metamorphosis*

Is it the drugs or is it me?
The walking trees come from a tram
the size of several hundred dogs.
A morphine glade. (Unscheduled stop.)

Curiouser. The pain is veiled –
a hard look misted but not missed,
an apiarist in white mourning.
Through its window I can see:

someone's pet – a flat disaster –
serene on the stared-at pavement,
linked by a red and scribbled cord
to an impastoed daub. (What's *that*?)

And curiouser, among the trees,
a plant holds up her falling face
and draws apart. Phones hang about
the bearded oak, my dear master.

iv *81 Sturla Road*

Poor world, the violet insect-o-cutor glow
of streetlights on the fallen snow is something like
my need of him who sleeps nearby, but mostly not.
Mostly it is itself as cars search roundabouts
and underpasses on a mid-December night,
the quiet mine, the stealth of my approaching joy.
The superstition I am felt before I'm seen,
trudging along the hummocked road towards one door,
leaving behind the death of heretofore – that's life.
Some curtains aren't yet drawn. Unfaring families
look out and mark the grey, possible cat. The Wierd.
He is the shape of long but not forgotten fears –
of thrall and invasion, the wolf, the brand, the flame
striking the thatch; old ghosts in a new territory.
The air clears. By a hole-punched moon I see a ream
of false prospects, the other world, white, coining it.
Visible breath, tonight, give me no miracle,
no six zeroes, but just a step, the ultra-blank
inheritance of those who leave and then come back.

The Turn

Under the sign
of Worthington are bolts
of cloth that will be cut
before Victoria dies.

The road, not empty but
not full, climbs Anerley Hill,
the palace a swim bladder
from an alien cetacean.

Seven miles north,
a girl shapes letters
as the light thickens
to match her slate:

her name, her age, how
many she would like,
some names for them.
So young, so toothless,

mother of my mother – still
an egg in that girl's larder
wobbled by the wobbling
cartwheels overhead

and me a fluke in its vitellus,
smoky as the tailor's breath
on backing for a waistcoat
he will wear dancing.

North marries South,
a hand clasps silk — a feel
of consequence to it now
that the Queen is dead.

Puzzle for Christopher

Q: Please write me a sonnet on the subject of the Forth
Bridge.
A: Count me out on this one. I never could write poetry.
– Alan M. Turing,
'Computing Machinery and Intelligence' (1950)

'The stated world can be recalcitrant
And yet its knottedness will often yield
To inspection, depending on the terms
You use, as they are heard and redefined.
I do not wish to give the impression . . .'
(How unlike yours my calculated sound.)

You don't reply, suspecting encryption
Perhaps, or, being dead, absent of mind.
I am in touch with other men. I grieve.
I dreamt that I was you again last night,
Played noughts and crosses on a page I keep
Beside my bed, where in the early light

I saw Euclidean parallels converge.
The sense in which I speak's provisional;
Dawn sends my message to a why-station
Which strips out interference, bird by bird.
Because of you I'm rarely lost for terms,
Untying knots. But never say a word.

IV LIVE RECORDINGS

> . . . I have learned some secrets of life which are now
> dimmed in my memory by the operation of that same law
> which ordains that the convalescent, once cured, ceases to
> understand the mysterious truths laid bare by illness, and that
> the prisoner, set free, forgets his torture, or the conqueror,
> his triumph passed, forgets his glory.
>
> – Marguerite Yourcenar, *Memoirs of Hadrian*

He took a history, diagnosed my problem (a tilted and rotated pelvis) and spent an hour and a half making little rolling and kneading moves up and down my back and my legs before teaching me to stand up. I have been favouring my right leg for years. He perceived, somehow, that I'd been anxious and angry, and anxious about being angry; that I harboured, as he put it, 'fiery thoughts' which (of course) affected my behaviour towards others but found an equal expression in dreamlike self-recriminations. His treatment rooms, above a newsagent, were unkempt to the point of squalor. The Balmain Therapy Centre has no shop front, to put it mildly: no calming music, no ornamental arrangement of willow sticks in an amphora, no green tea. Robert McCusker works in a musty apartment with yellow blinds, no carpets, no light, a padlocked toilet and rooms containing single mattresses on faded floral divan bases. His clothes were clean but he smelt of smoke. Before becoming a Bowen therapist,

Mr McCusker was an engineer. He described circulatory problems as an engineer might, making reference to fluid dynamics and hydraulic systems. He also spent some part of his life designing toothbrushes: there were a few examples (still in their packaging) on the wall above a couple of pages of A4 on which were printed some not quite grammatical affirmations about living a life of possibility and being kind. He did not take card payments. He had no cash register or box. He didn't mention money. I told him I had a hundred bucks with me. The physiotherapy practice I'd called the day before charged 'between $200 and $250 for an initial assessment'. Robert McCusker told me to walk up and down the length of my friend's house for one minute every half hour for the rest of the day and then, starting tomorrow, to walk for half an hour every day for the rest of my life. He didn't do anything with the hundred bucks I put on the table. He shook my hand three times before saying goodbye and wishing me well. 'Your pelvis is pretty much level now and I think you'll find you're not as anxious.'

★

People who emigrate quite early on in life and adopt a new language still speak to dogs in their mother tongue, even if it is one they have for the most part forgotten. Something interesting is happening. Speech is a higher brain function, a result of the evolution of the cerebral cortex, but the mother tongue, as the term suggests, is that part of the function that is nearest to the mammalian brain where emotions and concern for others (including other creatures) and for the young originate. So when we speak to dogs in our mother tongue, we are not being soppy. We do it because our limbic system has recognized Dog, and with it the pre-human mammal. We do it *without thinking* because we are reaching very quickly for a way of responding to a signal transmission – a communication – that predates thought. The signal is not a language, but it has information to which we respond. We have received a message we can't open. *Pace* Thomas Nagel, of course we don't know what it is like to be a dog, or to form a concept of what it is like to be a dog; but our instinctive deployment of an abandoned human language in front of one suggests by potent analogy that our mammalian brains did know, once.

★

Anne or Anna spoke so brilliantly about the Chinese economic model that I was reduced to awed silence. I said something, anything, in reply and she nodded enthusiastically. One rarely understands the specialisations of another. Is politeness the pretence that we do, or a sign we don't?

★

What a tough little book *Pride and Prejudice* is. It turns out that the romance isn't the heart of the book. The heart – the emotional lesson that keeps having to be learnt – is the realization that in order to choose someone for a partner, however good he or she is, however good you may wish to be yourself, you will have to disappoint others and, very possibly, make them miserable. This is what stating a preference of any sort involves, and it is as true of the most heartfelt affections as it is of decisions based on economics. Fitzwilliam Darcy disappoints Lady Catherine de Bourgh, her daughter, and Miss Bingley. Jane Bennet disappoints Miss Bingley. Lizzie disappoints Miss Bingley, her father, and possibly Jane. Lydia disappoints everyone except her mother. (The proof of this schematic reduction is in the clear view it affords of Caroline Bingley's central and pitiable isolation in the novel – something we feel, something that burns under the surface comedy.) It is almost as though Austen were saying: there are no unalloyed generous actions. Those who are pleased for others are made happy by their actions for selfish reasons, because the actions of others happen to suit them, and selfishness by extension is no more or less than the propensity in others not to behave in the ways we would prefer.

★

I had a vision of the anger and grief and fear that had bedevilled me staring in amazement from the open top of a stuffed backpack left lying on the corner of Sydney and Glenlyon Road where the trams stop. The emotions were amazed to discover that they hadn't been holding on to me: I had been carrying them. Then they disappeared. I felt as I do when I come across a fresh pint of milk in a fridge I'd thought empty. Unencumbered. I looked again from my window and saw no backpack on the corner of the street, only a few bees zooming in and out of the rosemary. The emotions were gone.

★

Powerful spouses often go to pieces when their compliant partners die, because the compliance turns out to have been a permission to behave powerfully, and in death that permission is revoked.

★

A long medical discussion may easily become an organ recital.

★

Even when it is used benignly, in the context of a brave but trivial act − like asking someone out on a date − 'nothing to lose' is a phrase I don't really like. It refers approvingly to an absence of pride and expectation. One isn't holding back, being guarded. But not having too much pride doesn't mean one shouldn't have expectations. Expectations are normal and a part of social identity, of being held to others' meanings, as Hegel and many others have believed. Without them, we see quickly how having 'nothing to lose' can tip some people over the edge of an obscure precipice into troubled waters of unawareness, where their actions are dwarfed by the void; where the lack of social significance (of expecting to count socially) leads in a strange loop to diminished responsibility and a fantasy of hidden power. Thrown back on its own resources, the unremarked ego is like a very massive particle in some singular early-universe crisis: with nothing around it to provide limits, the particle undergoes a kind of maddened inflation − filling everything. The typical psychopath is a solipsist, all-powerful and at the same time socially deleted. Whatever happens to others is part of that social deletion: 'nothing'. In perfectly normal circumstances, too, intimations of mortality shadow the usage. 'What's stopping you? What have you got to lose?' means 'What is the worst that could happen?', and behind all the possible answers to those questions – my pride (again), my job, my marriage, the house, the kids – all serious, but all conformable to a sense of what is not fatal – lies the unspoken end-answer, which is always 'Well, I could die'. And in truth this isn't just a possibility: it is a certainty. Of course, it is unlikely *for now* in most cases where the question is asked, and so unlikely as to promote feelings of relief on the part of the respondent. But couched in that relief are two significant things: one is the reminder that, on the contrary, one has everything (one's life) to lose – though not yet; and the other is that one is a person to whom collateral losses are also insignificant, because one is somehow essentially middle-class, and even in a crisis the means to get by will appear. It is a terribly creepy phrase. One would not use it in a) the trenches, or b) the company of a single mother who has just, finally, found a flat.

★

I bought the tortoises to teach my nephew and niece about death, forgetting that tortoises live to be about 150. Really what tortoises teach you about is abusive relationships. When they're small, their amphibian gender isn't clear. What you want in any case is two females. They will get on quite happily, eating lettuce, burying themselves, chatting in their box after lights out in their soft leathery voices. Two males will kill each other. And one male and one female are almost as bad, it turns out, because the male will fuck the female to death. This wouldn't happen in the wild, where the females live in harems and are spared the constant attentions of any one hormonally demented male, and where (crucially) they can escape. But in captivity, one on one, the woman doesn't stand a chance. The bull bites her neck and her knees so that she can't run off and then fucks her all day and all night until she's a sad little ghost trailing about the borders of your garden with a bit of cabbage leaf draped over her head for camouflage and protection.

★

Criticism ought to be succinct and simple and it is no easy thing to be either. We are led away from what we think by a flow of associations, mental and verbal, and by the desire to appear intelligent, or at least interesting. In fact, the succinct and simple observation will always be interesting because it is likely to be honest, saying: this is what I've found. The coating of difficulty and self-display worn by much criticism is there to disguise the fear that what the critic has found does not amount to much: 'I like *Pride and Prejudice* but it is galling to see it fawned over by people who so clearly seek the society of a classic'; 'I think the speakers in the Old English elegy "The Wife's Lament", and Elizabeth Bishop's poem "Filling Station", are both dead'; 'I admire a lot of modernist literature without knowing what it is about'; 'I imagine most poets, in secret, would agree that good formal verse is poetry and the rest is often rubbish.' Also, it is a bit rich for me to complain about critics wanting to appear clever when I have invested considerable time and energy in contriving just that appearance myself; whereas, mostly, I read something and my mind is a blank, for a long time, until the old need for approval and the old fear of disappointing prompt speculation. A faint echo of mortal panic induces me to put words down. Then I might consider that the blankness and the animated moment of misgiving belong together and together make up my inner critical life, which is not a crowded landscape but something like an empty shoreline occasionally intruded on by footprints or crabs.

★

Theirs was a difficult house, hard enough to live in if you knew how it all worked, and impossible for guests who didn't. The owners would tell you what you needed to know – where the frying pan lived, the knack for closing the bathroom door – though always with a little exclamation of surprise, and irritation ('Oh! Didn't I tell you?') that conceded the oddity of their domestic arrangements (broken beds, bare light fittings, crumbling plaster) and scolded you for drawing attention to it.

★

I like looking out of windows. Life narrows to a point. Slowly I empty myself into the sea, a curve in at least four dimensions. There is a point to this, and it is a mathematical pattern. The pattern is the porthole mind, the O through which one falls, or pours, perpetually.

★

The arrival of the Fair did not coincide with any obvious holiday – maybe a Bank Holiday weekend, maybe not. A secret timetable, or maybe something in the soil, governed its overnight appearance. Suddenly it was there, with a sweet smell of diesel from the hot generators and sugar from the candyfloss spinner settling over the park like a witch's spell. The Fair was a rough place, for reasons that were never fully explained – something to do with types and thieving – and I had to go in a throng, with friends who were somehow not my normal friends, most of whom were tougher and braver than me. I stuck to the penny roulettes and soft toy stalls. Most of the rides scared me, though worse than the rides was the dread of being forced to go on one or, worst of all, made to confess that I couldn't, I didn't dare, I was too scared. It comes down to control. I liked the Dodgem cars because they were earthbound, not flying about on the end of rusty pistons, and they were under my control, sort of. There was a rudimentary steering wheel. My friends liked the thrusting, accelerating horrors – the flying cars, the centrifuge, the Waltzers – for the opposite reason: they had no control over them at all. You got on, someone pressed a button, and that was that. Only now does it occur to me that a preference for one distraction over the other said – says – something about both one's apparent attitude to life and, perhaps, one's real attitude to it. To the child behind the wheel, freedom is the retention of a personal influence over events. To the child pinned by gravity to the walls of a whirling drum, it is the exhilarating removal of that influence. My friends really liked being out of control. I didn't. Both situations, in miniature, could be said to exemplify the response of a particular personality type to the problem of choice, which is the problem of free will versus determinism, with disco in the background. But, looked at again, with a wider camera-angle, pulling back a bit to get the whole deafening field in shot – and it is actually quite a small space – both situations invoke, and are shadowed by, their opposites. I put my hands on the steering wheel, because I am driven to do so by the utterly unacceptable nature of all other choices (the centrifuge, the Waltzers), and my friends are flung about by a crude tangle of forces and programming, but only because they've willingly embraced it. Asked for it, as the saying goes. Volition and submission, circumstantially, require each other, and what disappears in all this is not free will or determinism so much as a preference in the order of events, in any given situation, for one over the other – and with that, too, disappears the illusion of there existing personality types who are much braver than X, more timid than Y. Life hides its fairness.

★

Poetry is the discipline exerted on or by words in order to summon feeling, often very painful feeling, at will. It is powerful because it recognizes that the material world, as far as humans are concerned, exists in psychological flux: no material or brute fact is an island. It survives in an atmosphere of witness. The blackbird I hear singing in the garden is a bird that has been heard. And though 'discipline' might suggest correction of some kind, it also suggests salutary habit and through the lens of this second sense we see a more helpful version of the first. The messiness of the world as it presents itself to creatures of emotion becomes subject to ordering, but the aim of poetic ordering is not to deny the emotion or regulate the world: it is to stabilize both in a form of words – an incantation, Thom Gunn says – that faces the entirety of the mystery, of why we are here to see and hear and locate these things in every daily particular. Such a facing up to the world requires self-discipline, also, and from the traces left in the poem by such self-discipline on the part of the poet we are comforted as readers. In its Latin root, 'comfort' means 'with strength': the idea is not to cosset the reader or to say, in any variety of naïve or so-phisticated ways, 'there, there'. It is to enable us to stand side by side with difficult experience. To withstand.

*

The word that haunts Thom Gunn's late-early collection *Moly* (1971) is 'live', the adjective, not the verb – the word on vinyl LP sleeves that tells you this particular record-ing of a band isn't a normal recording but something half-way to actuality, a kind of nearness to the real thing, the thing that's out of reach. In Gunn's poetry, it announces a coming-to-awareness that is of its time and place in the culture of sexual and gay liberation then flowering in San Francisco and New York. But its meaning, here, is beauti-fully snagged with metamorphic barbs, textures and surfaces, as if the poet were emerging from some classical cocoon of learning, not losing a disguise but, rather, watching himself shed a layer of inhibition or restriction. In the first poem in the collection ('Rites of Passage'), the speaker is a man–Pan amalgam: 'Behind an almond bough, / Horns gaudy with its snow, / I wait live, out of sight'. The rhythm of the stanza is a trimeter, rhymed *abcabc*; 'live' is and isn't stressed — as if the satyr described isn't alive *yet*, or is camouflaged by the newness of the season, the freshness of the sensation, which is highly erotic though not explicitly sexual. It's a poem about coming into one's body, about youthful potential and succeeding the father, the orthodox; about cruising: the ambiguous sexual object for whom the speaker waits is, at this stage in the Gunn biography, a woman who is 'really' a man. But it's also about the real 'live' nature of anticipation, which is exquisitely mental. The woman is a consort of the poetic imagination who is the herald of a man.

★

It is something to find a new, favourite tree, and I've found it: *Liquidanbar styraciflua*, a fine specimen of which grows in the Royal Botanic Gardens, Melbourne. A Mexican native, its tall trunk, roughly the colour and corrugation of a mature ash or walnut, branches out in irregular patterns and directions at (very roughly) ten-feet intervals. Unlike an ash, the trunk doesn't fork: the main mast stays intact. The branches are long, tapering gradually into leaf-heavy fingers you can pull and tug, feeling the whole vast limb behind the fingers respond with the lazy sway of a rope-bridge.

★

The word 'carriages' is lovely and minatory. In a carriage one feels the relief of being in transit, between two places, temporarily excused one's territorial responsibilities. That feeling is kin, also, to being transitory, with the vital difference that our transitoriness confers on us an immense responsibility. These are all the feelings and precious obligations we will ever have.

★

U. A. Fanthorpe's much-anthologised poem 'The Sheepdog' is subtler than it seems. It is a short dramatic monologue which, like many such monologues, begins *in medias res* to emphasise its overheard, unfaked quality, although the poet is also making a sly point about the paradox of Incarnation: the God in whom she believes and who made all things (including this dog), whose birth we are celebrating, has no remembered beginning and no end. The poem is, in addition, a study of generosity and the limits of self-awareness – of consciousness. A dog, very briefly, describes the events leading up to the Shepherds' departure for the Nativity and then the scene itself, based on what it has heard from the Shepherds on their return. The clear implication is that the shepherds, while realizing that Shep is an intelligent animal – *Stay, Shep. Good dog, stay* – have not been conversing with it as an equal. Of course not. For them, it doesn't possess language; it has a set of behaviours to which they attribute some vague but helpful quasi-mental states, such as instinctive loyalty, and so on. They are but men (to paraphrase Wittgenstein, 'if a dog could talk we would not be able to understand it'); and, of course, Shep is not speaking to anyone, either, but for different reasons. He is thinking aloud, for our benefit, which – if we follow him

– makes us, his readers, clever dogs, too. He does absolutely understand what the Shepherds have been saying about the Kings and the presents and the baby, and he is shamingly, magnificently 'unaware' of the odd imbalance in his relations with humans: that he gets them, perfectly, while they do not really get him. The possibility of a distinctive, world-jarring animal consciousness is comically indicated by the fact that this Judaean dog thinks in a broad Yorkshire accent. The 'thought' accent further reminds us that *our* human consciousness has a personal accent, too: an irreducibly real subjective component, which can't be got at ('heard') from the outside. Any amount of behavioural evidence for it is not proof that it exists. The proof is of a different order of phenomenological experience. It is a point of view. But having that point of view need not bind us to *one* point of view alone. We give other humans the benefit of the doubt. We allow the truth of our subjective conscious experience – what it's like for us to feel hungry, to see sunlight striking the figure in the carpet, to touch this paper or read these words – largely because it is attested and confirmed by others. Others, with comparable if not exactly identical experiences, know what it is like for us to feel hungry, or sad, or left out, or left behind; and we credit them with that understanding because, as the logician Alan Turing pointed out, we do not want to seem ridiculous, or solipsistic, and 'it is usual to have the polite convention that everyone thinks'. Shep, who understands us, gets no credit for it: he is not a part of that polite convention. We are narrowly self-aware, without being aware of him. His inter-species awareness, on the other hand, is subtle and penetrating and undetained by our limitations or any thoughts of unfairness. He bears a god within him, who is all quick perception, so quick as to be unthinking, and shockingly selfless.

★

The moment in which we speak and the moment in which we write are different. Words lead us astray in a spoken argument: the context evolves in dialogue, and our original intentions to say X, or make a point about Y, are lost or transformed. We have greater notional control on the page, because we are not conferring, not speaking aloud, but a conference still exists, internally, between possible ways of expressing something. And what we write always surprises us, because it has more in it of a peculiar, spoken slipperiness than we'd anticipated. (Forster: 'How can I know what I mean until I see what I say?') The acknowledgment of this inevitably retained slipperiness is what exercises the authorities, of course. Authoritarian authorities, especially. However many people toe the line and speak the official speech, it never sounds as if they mean what they're saying, because the saying has a different tonality from person to person. This is why dictatorships become paranoid: tongues harbour nuance. The ideal interlocutor in official language is either a group, a crowd, in which a mean tonality can be fleetingly established, or a prisoner, i.e. someone who has no voice. Actual individual voices are, by contrast, crowded with competing intonations, keys and pitches. Here, in addition, is the explanation for the blandness of official art. One crowd sounds like another. It takes singular art to imitate one voice.

★

I don't miss you yet, because you're still in the car.

★

Madame Bovary includes some audacious leaps of focus in a single scene – from characters observing action at one remove to the actors themselves – that are reminiscent of Chekhov's stage innovations, his concurrent conversations, the sense one has everywhere in the plays of a roving microphone picking up gossip. But Flaubert is writing in the 1850s, and his first novel was published in 1856, four years before Chekhov was born. Still, the playwright must have learned from it later on. Everyone does. Because this is the great novel of the heard before the said, that appalled emphasis on listening which is the secret of gripping dialogue. What other novel has the same acoustical daring, or the same terrifying presentation of sound, which catches us mid-sentence like the telltale scratching in a priesthole? (Rodolphe and Emma on the second floor of the Town Hall listening to the dignitaries speaking below; Hippolyte's scream in the distance when the surgeon has to amputate . . .) The technique is at its most dazzling in the last fifty pages, as Emma unburdens herself to Binet, the tax collector. She pleads, but . . . wait, there's a problem with the mike. We're losing you, Emma. We can't hear you. The story leaps from the room in which she is making her desperate suggestion to the attic across the street where the two avid gossips, Mmes Caron and Tuvache, are watching events unfold. We hear Binet's appalled response to Emma's offer, but not the offer itself. And we hear, too, the women conferring, their cruel delight. Emma is the focus of everything – the novel is *about* her, it closes in on her – but she has no voice, no point of view. The scene's two vantage points are like a pair of hands around her neck; and, sure enough, when we next see her, she is with Mme Rolet, Berthe's wet nurse, gasping for breath.

★

Along one stretch of the Upfield bike path is a long hoarding of gig posters for local venues and bands called things like It Had To Be Ewe or Bits of Shit. Purple morning glories have meanwhile spread themselves over the fence separating the path from the railway. They are from another age, the pre-ironic age of flowering plants. They straggle and pout like M. Jagger.

★

Sensibility is a difficult and subtle concept. The philosophical and aesthetic meanings that attach to it have shifted over the centuries, but it seems still to indicate something useful and interesting: emotional capacity or, as the OED puts it, the 'faculty for feeling' as opposed to rationality and sense. It seems to recruit inclining adjectives – gay, feminist, political – that tautologise, muffling the central idea that sensibility is in itself an inclination of mind and feeling, something that describes our way of looking at things, rather than (or as much as) the things – sex, gender, politics – themselves. Sensibility is sensitive to inspection. If overstimulated, or taken too seriously, it becomes an affectation (this was the core of eighteenth- and nineteenth-century objections to the literary and artistic cults of feeling) and with the modern addition of irony may even become a refuge from feeling, a sort of camp. Now, campery is fun, but it's also a code, a two-tiered theatricality where what one loves to display is pitched against what one really feels. Only fellow possessors of the code can unlock its full meaning. And so it's oddly hard to write campily, in a non-theatrical genre, because writing itself is not a particularly demonstrative activity: a camp novel can feel like a private joke that has outstayed its welcome. There aren't an enormous number of successful examples – the works of Ronald Firbank? Some of Brigid Brophy? Can we arrive at, for instance, a 'gay sensibility' that is identifiably gay, and public – even mainstream – at the same time? I have different answers to this on different days. A lot of writing by gay men and women has wrestled with this problem. How much can I disclose of who I am and what I get up to, what I think? How much do I even want to disclose? The primal necessity of making some kind of noise to assert one's existence – giving voice to one-self – rubs up against the requirements of art, which are paradoxical and come down to the liberation of meaning by formal constraint: shape, symmetry, grammar, story, framing, dialogue. We need the formality of agreed meanings in order to be understood. We also need to feel that we've brought some kind of personal nuance to those meanings. This is the give-and-take of every relationship in writing – and it's written into the title of Jane Austen's first published novel, *Sense and Sensibility* (1811). Readers may still assume the presence of an opposition in the title, but no: the novel is saying the faculty for reason and the faculty for feeling belong together. It asks: what can sense (Elinor Dashwood) bring to sensibility (Marianne Dashwood); and, equally, how can one sister's robust, Augustan sense of duty be made more flexible by the other's emotional capacity? How can a desire to express what one feels be shaped, not caged, by design? Chekhov returns to this subject in his short story 'The Black Monk' (1894), in which a mentally exhausted academic chooses maddened authenticity over conformity. It's a terrific tale, but a false antithesis.

★

On my second visit to Robert McCusker, he asked me if I was walking for half an hour a day, and I said I was, and I asked about other exercises I should be doing and he advised me to 'stick to the walking'. I made passing reference to the affirmations beneath the toothbrushes, the A4 print-outs about living a life of possibility and being kind, and he looked suddenly vague, a little red, not bashful, but uncomfortable. He said they had nothing to do with him. They belonged to The Landmark, the educational charity with whom he shares office space. (I can't see him sharing office space with an educational charity: there are old clothes lying around, a drab leather-effect sofa, and a telly with dials.) Then it occurred to me that this is how kindness might be spotted – in people who want nothing to do with it. I found myself recalling a grimly funny short story by Shirley Jackson – surely a tautology, since all her stories are like this – in which a kindly old lady, Miss Adele Strangworth, loved by so many, sits at home and writes malicious anonymous letters. The point to grasp is that she is not a hypocrite. Jackson's insight (it is one of her pet subjects) is that evil triumphs not when none resist it, but when it does not suspect itself of being evil – and this shrewd categorization of wrongdoing excludes the merely wrathful or intermittently self-deceiving, in whom some vexation of the spirit implies a degree of self-awareness, however warped or misguided. No, the real rotters are possessed – by serenity. More: a perfect self-possession is no less a form of possession than its demonic variety, and that is probably why Mr McCusker looked so haunted when I prodded him about the can-do affirmations. It is a vaguely disturbing dilemma: we can't be properly kind without being unselfconscious to a degree (a planned kindness has too much of ego in it to be kind), but an involuntary kindness, a kindness that is somehow not ours, is equally implausible: how can we take credit for it? Probably there is only one acceptable race of beings who are exemplary in their conduct and pursuit of principle while remaining beyond the reach of appeal and argued circumstance. And they are looking after the sheep.

V NO TRESPASSERS

Gang Warfare

after Thomas Hardy

'Go on, try.'
But the boy is coconut-shy
   To say nothing of his fear of taking aim
   With an unshoulderable gun. In flame,
Shaking, ready – almost – to die,
The sun watches, lowers its one red eye-
   Lid and melts slowly away.
Three goes. 'Can't lose,' says the woman with rings.
   But it grows chilly at the end of the day.
A husk rattles and falls softly among other things.

She will be there all week, perhaps longer,
   Fronting an inexhaustible supply
   Of stuffed tigers and other crap prizes,
Not getting any younger while the younger
     Players appear the same:
     Idly intrigued by such an innocent game
   Of rods and hooks and hoops of different sizes.
They are tempted, for whatever reason
   Empties a gun at coconuts, a shy
boy – one of, yeah, twins – or the sky, even.

The Half of It

A hot child sees itself and cries.
The kind face kissing through the glass
Perhaps half wants the things to come
To be the things already done,

Like thank-you letters. *I was home*
By eight! I had a lovely time.
Can you believe how much he's grown?
'Train gone,' he says. He weighs a ton.

Back in the car, the calm's a front.
Cumulative embarrassment
At having bought a foreign make
Glues pink parents to grey plastic

While their home-grown self-scrutineer
Flops sideways in the Honda's rear.
Sometimes the gone are gone for good.
Then others step out of the shade

To hold and kiss and separate
A hot child in the glassy light
From smiles that say, we lied, it's true.
It doesn't mean we don't love you.

Awake in middle age, I hear
The sound of life measuring mid-air
The muffled pulse, snow-falling slow,
Of things half done that come and go.

A Wedding

It's cow parsley, a weed not fully out.
It's not the countryside. It's Brockwell Park.
It feels as if it hasn't rained for days
And I'm aware of rain for the first time
Inside the Castle, snapped-off railings round
My childish den, the falling-wall forest,
A ruin crammed with cauliflower ears,
Craning, cloud-stuffed. Listen, the park's
Not the Castle, I know. The hooded crows
Bathe in a puddle ringed by managed scrub
And bluebells. They are queuing up to douse
Themselves before returning to the field
To dry, and there they contemplate the sun.
Some bark occasionally, straight-backed soldiers,
Each bird its own self-restored garrison.
They're used to this allowed freedom (am I?),
The long, remembered and rewarded wait
For locked doors to fall open with a shout.

Dandelion

Skies cross my window with the sound off;
below a sprung herb shudders at life-speed,
rewound; upstairs letters joined in silence
from a man who was involved but hit upon
a delicate code to tell me of his New Year's Eve
at Graubünden, 'firework amazing, very long'.
In a drawer of old bills keys to rooms

that stay unlocked. Books everywhere, of course;
among them voices raised and heard, never alone,
the ones married to harp and flute. And luck.
Which of the psalms will hear the clouds as
they pass overhead, a stave of wires their nest?
What makes them beautiful? Why do they tear
themselves apart like ageing stars or clocks?

A Likely Story

The object of this exercise is not to attempt the task of defining probabilities, but to provide a way in to assessing the respondent's perception of priorities and possibilities in his or her life.

Here are a number of statements-in-threes. Have a go at ordering each group of three, and feel free to annotate your choices or express reservations. There is no right order. What will seem obvious or important or applicable to some may not be so to others, and it may be felt that a strong element of fanciful or magical thinking is involved in many of the statements.

The order of preference is the starting point for a discussion.

i *At Home*

If I lived with excruciating pain, I would not be able to cope.
If I become ill, I still try to eat properly.
If I can just talk to someone, I ought to be fine.

If the house is clean, I feel better.
If the house is sometimes dirty, I do not think it matters.
If I see a mouse in the kitchen, I call Pest Control.

If my neighbor has a fall, it means extra responsibility for me.
If I have to do small repairs, I worry about bigger things.
If my partner had an affair, I could get over it in time.

If I am feeling low, I avoid official correspondence.
If I'm happy, I mind less about money and bills.
If there is an unexpected knock at the door, I freeze.

ii *At Work*

I can learn difficult things as long as they are explained
properly.
My time is valuable even if I'm not paid for it.
It is too late for me to learn how to manipulate new
technology.

When people in authority smile at me, it's a rare but
encouraging sign.
Salary negotiations go better if you're physically attractive.
The powerful prefer people who will always be grateful to
them.

Letters after a name are evidence of something, I suppose.
It's important that I feel I'm doing a useful job.
I don't personally agree with what's happening, but I
daren't complain.

I have made important friends through my work.
I make mistakes, so I'm reluctant to judge others.
I do not see the point of trade unions.

iii *At Large*

A catastrophe grows more and more likely, so why recycle?
'Cultivate your garden' is a good rule-of-thumb.
I find it relaxing to think about outer space.

It pays to keep abreast of current affairs.
I vote out of habit rather than conviction.
If I get involved in local politics, I will end up on camera.

I am sorry for the poor but I think I deserve what I have.

My children are safer with me than at any other time.

It is OK to let the kids run wild once in a while.

Something will prevent the human race coming to an end.

It isn't always nice to say what I really think about the future.

Accidents can involve people who are good drivers.

Gargoyles

A congregation stalled and so alike
it could be from the same ancestral stock;
      trailing a line, hook-sad as pike –
looks leading out into the winter light

and public speeches that discount the cost
of private variance; the plain-as-dirt, the awful joke,
      agnostics giving up the ghost,
displays of gut feelings that don't feel right.

Mill Moon

And this is where the children would have worked,
Not hearing the stream for noise, for years.
And there the beech trees guard the taken gate's
Replacement air and no one says, 'Stop! Thief!'

Or sees anyone drop anything, or cares.
And here's a childish lunacy: that I
Am grown and fully spared, plucked free of briars.
And is this all the dark I have to fear?

La Padrona

Great spokes of darkness,
cypress shadows at sunset,
the trees themselves brushstrokes
that wheel and flow, dialling up
Santa Eufemia in the listening gaze
of citizens who've seen changes,
if not to this: a four-arched bower
decked with gardenias and braid
carried by boys becoming men
and heralded by itchy musicians
divorced from boyhood's effigy;
the incense and the nicotine,
the candles lighted, loitering
as overhead the hawk watches
Plaza San Sebastian fill up, girls
eyeing those who pant and sweat;
parents, a few unphonable women
wrapped in experience, perched
heron-like on dry fountains.

Café Historian

Fire whirled the Crystal Palace away
like a wild waiter harried by debutantes.
The smell lingers. Ashes stick to my shoes,
the damp city at my back, gherkins, fried food.

A man on his own, nodding, thrown as a knife,
says, 'Did I see the glass burst in the cops' faces?'
Two of them look over, tiredly. I could have been
a bolster in the balustrade for all the chance I stood

of true witness. But he was in the park already,
among the cedar candelabras, watching the smoke
in its under-rehearsed escapologist's straitjacket
come rolling and screaming through the wood.

Heat Life

Everywhere you look you see a mess —
Sticking-plaster remedies, the scuff of things distressed:
A closed system at closing time. Oh, place your final bets
And get out barely half of what you put in, dear, or less.
The dealer in the tumble-dryer shuffles as he sweats.
Some loss of socks continues even though he's fully dressed.

I could have kept quiet about all this,
But it takes energy to aim and energy to miss
A closed system at closing time. I'll place my final bets
And settle for a half of what I gave you, dear, a kiss.
The bookie on the rabid nag gets caught in his harness.
He'll hang on. What else can you hope to do in a crisis?

Hearth

I look into the small theatre of the fire
Where flames play something from a distant repertoire

And shape my loss. Someone has left an impression
From which a cast of words can nearly be taken;

Though words, the truth, and understanding aren't
   enough,
They're not nothing – footprints, definite hints of stuff

Thought softens at the edges like roofs in a drift.
I hear these logs squealing, the lid on your rice lift.

I see the point of distraction, far-starred effect
Whose spark-propelled advice to get real I accept

Quickly, and then forget. Help me, warmth, constellate
The night with glowing notices. Wasn't it great?

Physics

What is cold, dark matter?
Nobody knows: perhaps it is pleasure.
By any normal means of reckoning
In short supply and difficult to measure.

But we'll keep looking. We'll persevere,
Hotly pursuing its rumoured existence
Across sky-maps of myriad treasure
To the far plainer abundance.

The Claim

Track cradle divorced
from the trestle's top girders, sleepers
rotted, later ramblers' cairns

knocked down, insect feedback
like an infant moron's monotone
you've done it now um ummmmmmm

now glittering in the long echo
of rockfall, tottering dossiered shale,
some cruddy hematite

and on the shadier banks
beneath vine maple, spruce,
rock covered in moss and in the moss,

washed out, the patient flakes –
plectra, white scales – of gold.
A green garter slips through the trees.

Bears use this bridge; though they're
cautious they don't much dwell
on man-made frailty. They see

a way across the creek,
a road to food and shelter in the dusk
and high-thrown sugar of night.

How old are the trees?
Not old. The pines seventy at most,
the girlish birch counting back

thirty, twenty, ten, a choir
lisping the same old songs, not
knowing why they sing them.

Trees, bears, a snake, water and time.
What did those early passengers and trains
weighed down with ore think of the sign

that mushroomed in their tracks? *No
Trespassers*. Hardscrabble foretold?
The owner's warning, and no lie.

Maximes d'Azur

Young people in the water ignore the monster yachts.
Look at the arms dealer watching television! He loves
    Filipinos.

The staff at their own table consider the smoking lights
    and fish.
Who is the boy pirouetting on his mobylette? This is not a
    rodeo.

Ce n'est pas le rodéo, ce soir? (A perfume of her former self:
No need of parasols at night, no dark glasses for Jacqueline.)

The photographer stands where other photographers stood.
Close down the restaurant, let the stone pines drift inland.

VI THE INEVITABLE GIFT SHOP

The truth seems to be that we live in concepts of the imagination before the reason has established them.
– Wallace Stevens, 'Imagination as Value'

A mile from the deserted cattle station and Victorian dog pound, a steep path falls through tea-tree bushes, wattle and scrub to smooth pink potassium-rich granite around which the river bubbles and snakes. Up and down the bark of gum saplings runs a series of rippling reflections. Other trees are iced with an assortment of frilly-white, grey and peppermint lichens. Hot spells during the day alternate with much cooler ones when clouds, even light ones, pass over, and in the evening as soon as the sun sinks behind Sugarloaf. At about nine comes a temperature inversion as heavy mist presses down on the warmer air in the valley, and for a short while the smoke from the campfire will not rise and instead dribbles over the stone hearth like dry ice from a cauldron. The magical overflow has a bewitching effect on our happy gathering around the flames. No one says the word 'inversion' or alludes to the change, which is typically unexpected, but the conversation is interrupted, the original subject lost and in its place the mostly silent owner of the neighbouring plot begins a story that casts an unusual spell. Two surveyors, a master and his apprentice, are sent into the bush to scout a development on the fringes of the national park. The master's wife cooks them five meals for the five days they are away from home. She waves them off. They bring home the empty Tupperware boxes and thank her for the delicious food, not telling her that they in fact lived off grilled sausages and white bread for the entire week and fed the home-cooked meals to the dog. Later, the master is sent away again. The wife has had more than enough of her husband, but she waves a cheery goodbye as usual. Then she goes to the apprentice, with whom she has been having a wonderful affair, and tells him: the meals her husband has taken with him are laced with an untraceable toxin drawn from a buried side of meat. 'He will die!' she cries. 'I have poisoned him! We are free!' The apprentice goes white and has to sit down. That evening, in the soft-shouldered mountains, about a mile from a deserted cattle station, as the smoke from his campfire dribbles over the stone hearth, the husband eats his sausages and gives his wife's food to his dog. In the night, a grotesque gargling from the poor dog's corner wakes him. Meanwhile, far from the story-book national park but on the terrible, vertiginous brink of waking from something that is not a dream, the apprentice tells his lover the real fate of her meals and it is her turn to sit down. She knew, she knew, she realizes. How could she have known? A car with a spinning blue beacon draws up outside. We listen to this story in a semi-paralysis of excitement and revulsion, as though we and not the loyal dog had scoffed the *Clostridium botulinum*, and consider its teller, a wealthy lawyer who goes on to talk about a holiday in Calabria as though it were a prison sentence. He drove through working-class southern Italy with the windows down and 'couldn't wait to get the fuck out of there'. Is he in the heroic tradition, a man like

Odysseus or Beowulf whose tall tales add to his substance, or is he the ill-omened messenger? I can't decide. His wife looks at him and at her rather strong drink. He eats with his mouth open and stops every so often to take a breath, the food still on his tongue. He's like a big ginger Tom stuffed into a smaller cat's stripy shirt.

★

A lie requires so much peripheral detail, whereas the truth doesn't worry about motivation or setting or background history. Fiction aspires to the condition of truth but is vulnerable to detail – so eat nicely.

★

Lydia Davis's translation of *Madame Bovary* rises to the challenge of Flaubert's weirdly plain orotundity and catches the light like the fields of pasture and tillage at Yonville through which the river winds, or illuminates the way in which Charles's mother and Emma pacify each other so hollowly. But even the successes miss something. They are attempts to reproduce the balance of the original sentence and the result is a sort of cold neo-classical symmetry; what we don't get is the sense of a tongue, the speaking voice of the writer. This has always been the hard part of translation – to re-create for another language culture, the effect and meaning of the original's beauty. I wonder if it can be done any more. Isn't such recreation dependent on the idea that for every essentially French recognition of Flaubert's genius there must be an English equivalent rooted in a sense of Englishness, a tone that has something to do with nationality? Davis wants to 'capture' the formal beauty of Flaubert's diction for an English-reading audience. How is that even to be imagined? (It reminds me of Bernard Williams's riffs on imagining oneself as having been someone else. If all our mental and physical characteristics are transferable, what capturable quality, exactly, is being transferred?) An even better translation would leave the whole question of tonal fidelity alone – in part because, *pace* Davis, writers going on about their own interest in it are usually boasting about their greater sensitivity: it's like saying 'I'm funny'. Instant disqualification. We want not the 'French' shape of a sentence, but the sense of belongingness to English – a relationship to the rest of our English linguistic environment. It is a daunting task that few translators manage, because they have sworn to capture, not rewrite.

★

I spent half an hour trying to free a new spatula from the piece of sales cardboard that accompanied it. I didn't read the copy. I bet it screamed with laughter the whole time. The problem: cable ties. Cable ties are impossible to remove because they are ratcheted mechanisms with angled grooves that only pass through the 'buckle' in one direction, like clockwork cogs. Once the tie is caught, it can't uncatch. I said aloud, as so many have, 'what would a little old lady do?' In the dismal silence that followed, broken only by my curses, it dawned on me that a little old lady, and no one else, would know exactly what to do. And where is she when you need her?

★

We may have grown too used, after Pound and Carlos Williams and their limitless progeny, to the idea of the 'image' in modern poetry as a proof of clarity and right-perception. Mere speech acts, and argument that involves abstraction, seem in this light to invoke a rhetorical quality or breathiness. But of course we need to breathe in order to look, and in any rhetorical tradition it is the length of the ur-phrase, the breath, which determines what can be seen and said – the two are co-terminous. In the parcelling-out of breath we may hear the spoken origins of poetry and epic, but also of a dramatic necessity, suspense. The stirring opening to Milton's *Paradise Lost* is powered by a delayed verb, 'sing', which comes when the long first sentence's oxygen is already failing. The poem's first lines are a reminder of the Fall, dramatized here as an expulsion of breath that promises redemption (Christ's martyrdom, but also Milton's Republican exegesis); and this redemption will be as natural and politically inevitable as breathing, the poet claims. Spirit and breath are theologically cognate, after all: our spiritual breath has failed us and Milton asks God to inspire him, as He inspired Adam, to see what went wrong. To see aright – to go any further – we must breathe in once more.

★

Poetry, for T. S. Eliot, was famously the 'escape from personality', a lovely if somewhat opaque remark. It's easier to see what he means when he calls for a 'concentration' of impressions and experience at the point of creation – what counts is not the extent of our indebtedness to the emotions and feelings of prior experience (the autobiographical component) but rather the emotions and feelings that are synthesized in the moment of writing: the discoveries of writing itself. One wonders even so what happens to the personality doing the writing, from which the writing escapes. Perhaps another phrase can help us – 'He's lost in his work' – which we can imagine being said by some half-admiring, half-despairing partner or colleague. A compliment and an insult. Or even an expression of concern. The work, whatever it may be, is an act of self-conscious creation that has the effect of cancelling self-consciousness, and something is gained thereby. Capability and application outrun ambition and desire. One salutary distraction, skilled endeavour, drives out lesser anxieties. Loss becomes freedom: the mind is disciplined, the ego tamed. But the other meaning shadows that happy escape: the capability can become obsessional; it may have economic utility (if we imagine really hard) for the household, but it can become obsessional, and a too-exclusive devotion to it may result in a loss that is self-desolating. Dedication leads unexpectedly to suffering and perhaps distraction of the grimmer sort. I believe in magical danger. The hint of creative automatism in Eliot's remark – that poetry is done by persons who wish to escape personhood – echoes William Empson's alarming idea that one writes poetry in order to empty the mind. Much as I admire Empson, I think that's going rather far along the path of artistic submission. And yet it is absolutely true that one risks something by conducting experience and feeling on the page, and that emptiness is involved. What one risks is the sympathy of others, of course. They have your loss to deal with. They see someone in fugue. And they may be indefinably irritated. Because . . . what is special about your claim to be *writing*? The painter and the musician have skills: obvious refinements of dexterity that can be pointed out as the art happens. But in the literate age, everyone writes. The writer's ability is merely a claim. While it is being created, the work is occult – from *occultus*, or 'hidden'. It has no very extraordinary apparatus. It is an impersonation of anyone.

★

Dignity matters, but not that much, as I told the police officer on Clapham Common. It has the quality of a damnable virtue. We like Milton's Satan not because he is proud – pride does not allow itself to consort with other feelings and thereby forfeits our sympathy – but because he is unrescuably dignified. He knows the fix he's in. Undignified behaviour usually involves the pretence that we are still, really, dignified. When Ron Davies was arrested for having sex with a man on Clapham Common, he didn't bother pretending, or not for very long, and I felt that was reasonably dignified. Less dignified was the call I received from a journalist at the *Independent on Sunday*. He was interested in writing an article about where gay men went to have sex on the Common. He wanted to go down there and have a look. Where should he go? I told him. It isn't my business what he does to relax. Oh, but wait. He wasn't relaxing. He was working.

★

In the *Confessions*, St Augustine thought 'matter' almost nothing. In his lecture on Genesis 1, Luther disagreed. 'How can something with substance be nothing?', he asked. It is unfair to blame Luther for not knowing about the hydrogen atom (99.999999996 per cent of it is empty space). On the other hand, Augustine didn't know about it either, and he was right.

★

Something is more or less well done but it flows away from me in the doing, and when it's finished I feel often a mild perplexity at the thing done – at the idea that it had anything to do with me in the first place. Because there is no way back into the work as it happens. Much as we might rejoice in the escape from personality, we're apt to be disconcerted by the experience of liberation – by the irretrievable oddity of what we produce. How was this written, who wrote it? We can find in this perplexity an analogy to the problem of how the mind and consciousness arise from physical materials (molecules, neurons). I don't really see, as Daniel Dennett does, that the 'mind is the brain (properly understood)'; that consciousness is in the end describable as brain states. I side instead with anti-reductionists like Thomas Nagel and John Searle who think point-of-view is irreducible – that there is an 'ontologically subjective' component to conscious experience. Searle nevertheless maintains, with some difficulty, that subjective mental reality is a 'higher-order' property of the biological brain. He doesn't recognise the distinction between the mental and the physical, which must make for some interesting pillow talk, and claims instead that consciousness is the product of something he calls 'biological naturalism': 'consciousness . . . is caused by neurobiological processes'. Whereas Nagel believes that, since objectivity is a 'defining condition' of the interaction of the brain's physical parts, the subjective nature of mental reality will not ever be found in 'the details of [their] physicochemical operation'. What both thinkers want to nail is the Aristotelian consequence of neuronal activity, which we might call the generation of complexity. Simple actions have complex outcomes, which make those original actions irretrievable as parts of the descriptive process. The irretrievability of the original activity, like the post-hoc inaccessibility of the artistic process, is the thing to grasp. 'I've lost my keys' – the keys are materially as they were, and probably where you saw them last, but you can't find the fucking things. We are, as subjective beings, the products of a No Way Back paradox. I think that consciousness arises from purely physical processes, but a physicalist description of those processes cannot account for consciousness.

★

'Look what is best, that best I wish in thee: / This wish I have; then ten times happy me!' Through the concluding couplet of Shakespeare's thirty-seventh sonnet breathes the suspicion that the Friend may not be worthy of the poet's trust and affection (and indeed in sonnets 40–42 the Friend is directly accused of sexual treachery and as soon forgiven). But if he is not, so what? This is one of those inside-out Shakespearean themes – not simply that the lowly and the downcast are capable of great feelings (to which poetry does not add so much as do justice), but that the worthy often love the unworthy, who are ennobled by such love even when they scant it. Therein lies the pathos. Affection is not wasted, but its generosity may not be recognized and in a funny way perhaps even depends on remaining unrecognized. In which case, isn't it also a little vain? It's true: timidity often does have an air of angry self-congratulation about it. The secret lover, tender of his or her dignity but risking no lasting rejection, glimpses this self-love and acts to banish it with praise of the beloved that reinforces a sense of separation and resentment.

★

I eat fish with a clear conscience because they neglect their young.

★

Extras in action movies are always walking down the street on the phone and having their phone stolen by overpaid short men. How might this theft affect the phone's owner? Perhaps she was taking an important call – trying to ring the hospital where her son or daughter is critically ill. What if the short man with the nylon hair has unwittingly destroyed the life of the bystander? Who cares about the 'main plot', then? Sadly, you can't tell the bystander's story without making her a 'main character', too, and so severely limiting her moral stature. She would have to be doubly recast – once as the new bystander and once as the lead. It's a hard life.

★

The arrival of a postcard is more miraculous than that of a letter, because its size and the exposure of the words on the back are more obviously survivals (of the weather, of date stamps and inquisitive postmen, etc). It's a tile, a piece, a relic of a holiday, destined for the corner of a board or the back of a drawer. It's also the voice of everyone. We're not all confident or garrulous enough to write a letter, but many otherwise unlettered souls have felt moved to write a post-card. It's a duty, dashed off but loving: high emotion com-pressed by form without being constrained by formality. Special enough. And the voices are not just from Margate. They come from Ancient History as well, because postcards are really pictograms – pictures and words in one. They are tokens – as the clay seals of the city of Uruk were tokens – of a given moment and a certified exchange. I remember you. Now you remember me.

★

That something as uncategorisable and odd as music, which is neither language nor science, should mean so much to so many people in ways that are observably shared and also unique I take to be a strong proof of the metaphysical nature of reality.

★

I didn't get a chance to chat to you when you were in the office. I know how fond you were of stories about my aunt, the one who lived in Highbury. She now lives in a home, but doesn't seem to have changed much. Her delight is to ask the other old ladies at the home how old they are. They usually reply that they are in their late seventies or eighties, to which she responds: 'Blimey, I look much better than you do, and I'm ninety.'

★

On Cockatoo Island, a former prison and shipyard, there are cockatoos but mostly gulls – gulls on endless parade, red-beaked, nesting on the pathways, in the open, in corners. Inside the convict precinct I see butler sinks, painted stone walls (flaking but not badly), sunlight on somewhat restored wooden floors. Through a doorway into the galley the stirring sun reveals a 1960s gas cooker with Perspex dials, low formica units. (There is an invisible room next to this one, where a little old lady watches television with a boy in a grey school shirt.) The building's like a schoolroom; the galley belongs in a vestry. Where is the morning coffee? Where are the sissy deacons and wide women bickering about cups and saucers and biscuits? Where are the rows of children practising hymns? The old floorboards have the flattened nails of a million Victorian houses from Sydney to Sheffield. The cast-iron door has a trap-window for the delivery of slops – for the gaoler to look in. Outside, the birds are the convicts, the inmates loosed from one prison into another – the bodies of birds that are souls in flight, or not, as the case may be. They stand at angles to each other, shrieking. Two olive-green and black speckled eggs nuzzle the bottom of the guardroom door, which opens onto a precipice, the isolation cells having been demolished in the 1890s – when the little old lady was born – to make room for the Sutherland Dock. On the ledge are a few stone slabs, streaked with gull shit like vanilla slices baked by Heston Blumenthal. Also the reel for a missing fire-hose. The side of the guardhouse is a midden. Among the screaming gulls hops a one-footed duck, looking for seeds. The gulls are oblivious. Her stump has been beautifully bound; at some point she has been caught and cared for. She has a cloudy breast and throat dotted with soft charcoal, a grey flank and wings, and black tail-feathers.

★

The last three words of Sonnet 43, which is about perceiving rather than seeing the Friend, are reversible: 'all nights [are] bright days when dreams do show thee me'. The sense is both: 'show thee to me' and 'show me to thee'; the revealing dream is a genuine night vision (that shows thee to me) and the dream of poetry which, being read, discloses the poet's great love (shows me to thee) and spreads across the insensate world to penetrate all appearances. Throughout the poem, Shakespeare enlarges on the theme of visibility versus noteworthiness, reality and truth in art. Art's shadow is best understood as a filter: it focuses reality, reduces dazzle, and by exaggerating contrasts makes clear to us what we miss by day when we 'view things unrespected', as an undifferentiated mass. So it is not a shadow in any pejorative sense, no mere projection away from an original, but an extension leading back to it. 'When most I wink, then do mine eyes best see, / For all the day they view things unrespected; / But when I sleep, in dreams they look on thee, / And, darkly bright, are bright in dark directed.' According to one commentary by John Kerrigan, 'darkly bright' means 'blindly seeing', but this isn't really right. The last thing Shakespeare experiences is any kind of groping intuition: rather he has a revelation about the true nature of the physical. Dreams are real, as art is real; we see with the aid of dream-perception; and art, a kindred seeing-as-dreaming, is a lens sensitive to this dark light. It's a significant advance on neo-Platonic wrangling with ideal forms and misleading substance. Because Shakespeare isn't interested in stripping things away or making *ex cathedra* pronouncements about falseness. The veil of form, things in their brute state, deranging emotion and mystery are not obstructions. They are the moonlight. 'In dreams, my eyes are sharpest, seeing fully in the way art also permits me to see; guided by the darkness, its unknowing, and the salutary irrational.'

★

A cabbage white's flight path – a river finding its way to the sea, faster.

★

When Shakespeare coins a new word, he characteristically compacts several others; he rewrites not what he wants to say, but the language. In Sonnet 65, he imagines a time when the beloved Friend has grown much older – 'when his youthful morn / Hath travelled on to age's steepy night.' 'Steepy' is sheer and shocking and works retroactively to give the whole clause a mesmerizing topography. Youth's declining morning meets inclining night, the foothills of age; and the uplands encountered are not just steep, but something between sleepy and steeped: 'steepy' is a pun, a quibble and a neologism at once. The sea-whisper of 'steeped', from the verb 'to steep' or to soak in liquid, is the stroke of genius. Some immersion on high ground has taken place, and no ordinary immersion, but an inversion. For the mountain of age is soaked, becomes 'steepy' night, and is as deep as it is tall – a vale of tears.

★

'The Seafarer' has chosen his exile: this is what makes him an apt figure for the Devil in Conor McPherson's play, which borrows its title from the Old English elegy. The Anglo-Saxon poem is a consideration of adventure – the mental embarkation of a voyager across the waves. His seafaring is internal, psychological, but it is also very closely tied to action and the reality of the sea. He is a seafarer who thinks about seafaring. The poem, on a first reading, seems in addition to dramatise a too-familiar modern (artistic) anxiety: how can one act in the world and write about it at the same time? But the world of the poem does not recognize that aesthetic separation: to the Christian Anglo-Saxon temperament, reflecting, writing and seafaring are alike activities that require preparation, and which come prior to a change of attitude or state of mind and body; that is, they are not metaphors for the life journey that precedes the transformation of the spirit, but examples of it.

★

In Shakespeare's sonnets one hears the low note and echo of abandonment – by a lover, certainly (by two, possibly three, lovers in fact), but also by time. They are a journal of transition from youth to age, or semi-visibility, and a witness to the work of substitution for love – of art for love – that is the poet's solace and gain. It would not be fair to say that they're a sign of retirement: Shakespeare is not Montaigne, not yet. Rather, they speak as an actor speaks when the audience is restless, when he knows he can no longer be heard: with peculiar freedom and relief. He will not be denied. (You can tell the truth if it's in an aside that's likely to be disregarded.) The sonnets are the door that swings in an arc from the Elizabethan open stage to the cool interior of Jacobean contemplation. Both worlds are shown in turn, and both refused as the door swings back in the opposite direction. The poems sigh, creak and fall open on the threshold of the age. Neither public nor private, they show us our age, too – our baffled impatience with company, alone with a phone but in the middle of a virtual crowd, where we are offered and denied both the solitude and the society we crave. Additionally, they exhibit a little of what Penelope Fitzgerald, in her novel *Human Voices* (1980), calls the 'tranquil pessimism' of the Midlands, and maybe this is why the couplets – so proverbial and final, yet so concealing, like a teacher giving advice without quite saying what she thinks, or with the luxury of knowing she will *not* be understood – read like sealed verdicts, at once fatal and innocuous.

★

The couplet at the end of Sonnet 130 ('My mistress's eyes') – Shakespeare's attack on Petrarchan conventions and his defence of particularity – is one of his most enigmatic. 'And yet, by heaven, I think my love as rare / As any she belied with false compare.' Helen Vendler thinks 'she' means 'woman', in which case 'belied' becomes descriptive: 'I think my love as precious as any woman who has been misrepresented by false comparisons'. But if 'she' is 'my love' (the dark lady) and therefore the subject of the last phrase, then 'belied' must be active, and the sense is: 'I think my love as unique as any [man or woman] she has reduced to the level of the commonplace by means of her false, unfair comparisons'. The latter is surely more plausible when we think of the sequence as a whole and all its jealous mudslinging. A shadowy figure – the slandered 'any' – is implied; perhaps it is the youth of sonnets 1–126, in which case 130 returns us to the triangle first encountered in 40–42 and the dark lady has been giving a false impression of the Friend. The poet seeks a truce: he thinks his love (the dark lady) as rare (as incomparably herself) as any other lover she may have traduced by false or unflattering comparisons. Shakespeare says that comparisons are inevitably false because people and lovers are unalike – both the Friend and the dark lady are irreplaceably unique – but that this uniqueness is also paradoxically a common denominator, the thing that makes us comparable.

*

Pinocchio is carved from wood and he's alive. He thinks, walks, feels – the only thing is, he feels that he isn't alive enough. He becomes a boy when he stops wishing for an excess proof of humanity. The moral is that we also step fully into our lives when we abandon self-regard – a state that should not be confused with self-awareness, which Pinocchio already has. We're all self-aware *enough*, and alive *enough*, Carlo Collodi is saying, with a sinister laugh, did we but know it.

★

Alan Turing attended Ludwig Wittgenstein's *Foundations of Mathematics* seminars in 1936 and enjoyed a number of good-humoured exchanges with the philosopher. Turing probably enjoyed them more than Wittgenstein. In one conversation about error and common sense, he slipped in a decidability paradox that his logical combatant failed to spot: 'One can never know that one has not made a mistake.' If this is true, then one cannot in general know if one has made a mistake or not, in which case the sentence may be false; but if it is false, then one can know in general if one has made a mistake or not and the sentence becomes decidable, which means it could be true.

★

In the display window of the Betta Health Medical Centre on Sydney Road is a disconcerting manikin torso covered in trusses and support stockings. With no head and legs off at the knees you might reasonably need a bit of support, but need the whole effect be so Rocky Horror?

★

Loveliest of all the Old English elegies is 'The Wife's Lament' or 'Complaint', if you're fractionally less sympathetic. The speaker, a non-native inhabitant of the land in which she finds herself, has been abandoned by her husband, his mind (possibly) poisoned against her by gossip. The wife lives underneath an oak tree in the woods, and the rootless cave in which she squats illustrates both the reversals of earthly fortune (what Della Hooke, in *Trees of Anglo-Saxon England* calls the 'progressive deterioration' of man's estate) and the exposure to danger of the wife's situation as a woman cast out from society. It is important to remember that woods in the tenth century harboured real threats: wolves, boars, loss of direction, and also other humans in exile grown monstrous. The friendless man, the *wineleas mon* of Maxims I (found with the elegies in the Exeter Book), is the wolf, the grey one, as Jennifer Neville has pointed out (*Representations of the Natural World in Old English Poetry*). The wife's predicament seems hopeless, yet the moral downfall isn't hers, it's her husband's – the man swayed like a branch by rumour. (Granted, the verse is opaque: there is a chance that he has left her in order to protect her from the fall-out of a plot, but that seems unlikely.) She abides, in the space hollowed out by a rootless love, with a curious mixture of patience and indignation. Here we encounter a marriage of varied emphases and traditions. The oak is the desecrated chieftain tree of the pagan wood, the dwelling place of the accursed; it is also the focal point of a wilderness to which the Christian solitary repairs in search of enlightenment through confrontation with fear; and it is the Tree of Life, bringing renewal through suffering. Oaks in Anglo-Saxon England often marked physical boundaries. This one marks the boundary between the world and the spirit, is symbolic and actual, and underlines the fact that in the Anglo-Saxon world there's little distinction between nature and the supernatural. There is only creation and createdness – a sort of sublime monism. 'Old is this earthen room; it eats my heart', she says (in Michael Alexander's translation). 'I go myself / about these earth caves under the oak tree.' A space beneath the oak eats her body; she roams an earthy enclosure. She has died and been buried, but lives on as a mental-material ghost. In another context, Hooke tells us that the Tree Register records a 'hollow oak with a girth of 1,230cm at Bowthorpe, near Bourne in Lincolnshire . . . [and that] the cavity has been used in the past as a pigeon-house.' A cage for the bird-soul, too, perhaps. T. H. White has this to say about pigeons in *The Goshawk* (1951): 'They were hard to kill. Grey quakers incessantly caravanning in covered wagons, through deserts of savages and cannibals, they loved one another and wisely fled.'

★

At the memorial tea for Anthony, his nephew Mark called him 'happy'. Uncle Anthony was an architect turned town planner, and balletomane. The difficult one in the family. Highlights of the tea included a priest with a ponytail that seemed to swing of its own accord, like a happy asp; performances of Bach's first cello suite and Tchaikovsky's *Swan* by a tired but brilliant student who'd been out clubbing the night before and kept yawning; memories of the deceased's Peter Cook-ish ear for detail – he liked to be called Antoine, but only by overfamiliar people who'd called him Tony first; and anecdotes. For instance: Uncle Anthony once sent a friend to Paris to find out whether or not Anthony Perkins really had an apartment on the Champs Elysées. He did – on the eighth floor of a building. The friend walked up eight flights of stairs and read the small brass plate by the door but didn't knock. He was under instructions. Uncle Anthony just wanted the rumour confirmed. He also wrote a now untraceable pamphlet on public sculpture in inner Melbourne; designed the sets for a production of *Carmen* (models on display); wanted originally to be a ballet dancer (though spondylitis put paid to that); believed you could think by drawing, and that making models forced you to resolve problems in relationships of all kinds, not just the spatial variety. He was on friendly terms with the oboist of the Frankston Symphony who shopped with, and for, Anthony in his later years and wheeled him to the supermarket. These forays were mostly a disaster, as Anthony loudly refused all fruit and vegetables and seemed interested only in the biscuits and sugary drinks that were his comfort after Joe died. I felt nevertheless that Mark was right and that Anthony had indeed been a happy man – as happy, possibly, after Joe's death from Aids as before, who knows? Aspects of mourning are private, to be known only by the individual concerned. But that is true of the other emotions, too. I like the idea that 'individual' once meant indivisible, and that what we find in the working-out of grief is a passage back towards the whole, a difficulty others may know about but not touch, like the silliest satisfactions in a shared life that are, understandably, for us alone.

★

Portraits of us done by others are surprising: we see our-selves as others see us, from the outside. Surely a self-portrait should be different, more accurate, the self attentively delin-eating the self, but it is not. The self-portrait is even more surprising than the objective portrait because, it turns out — the painting says — we are not as we see ourselves, either. The surprise is not confined to the page or the canvas. It clouds our vision on waking. Its intimate acoustic fills the bedroom at night, when the pulse races for no reason and I lie in bed in the grip of a strange astonishment that I am feeling these things. I push up at the ceiling with my hands, turning my head to one side and then the other. These are the articulations of the reptilian brain. When my reptile forebear was in danger, he thrust forward or flicked his tail to prove that he could move. Or he stayed still and hoped for the best.

*

David is making swimming motions in the water in front of me, his face red with the heat, his shoulders shining. He is smiling. We are in Iceland, in the white-blue silicate pools of a spa, the other bathers lulled into silence by the comfort and beauty of their surroundings, apart from some five or six Vikings in plastic helmets clustered around the pool bar (the bar is in the pool, so that you can order without leav-ing the water) who are well on the way to being drunk. We have driven through the lava fields to get here — spiky plains of basaltic outflow a thousand years old at most. While the wife was lamenting, her husband was running from the eruption's red grin towards his bouncing boat, thinking 'what the hell have I done? It wasn't like this in the brochure'. When the Norwegians arrived, a quarter of Iceland was forested. Then the climate grew harsher and many of the trees were cut down anyway or nibbled by sheep. The sheep didn't last, either. Today there is just 2 per cent tree cover, but plenty of pretty dwarf birches, willows and lupins. The obvious problem is the dark winter. To give you an idea, the big inland architectural attraction is a greenhouse, known as the Garden of Eden. It is a sizeable greenhouse, true / and yet more Homebase than Kew. Eruptions are every five years. You have to be practical. The Edenic flora are not very rare and so somehow the more wonderful: tomatoes, a squash, a dusty succulent, a pansy and some struggling herbs. Our tour guide had that correct sarcasm which is a feature of the Icelandic temperament: 'Inside the Garden of Eden you will find the inevitable gift shop.' Didn't Marx say something similar? And Iceland is dangerous, no question. Last night, in the lateral sunshine, we visited the Volcano Museum, where there was a display about the eruption of Eldfell that devastated the little island of Heimaey in 1973. It buried half of the town, but the inhabitants fought back to save the other half. Diggers were flown in from the States to shift ash. Fishermen turned enormous hoses on the advancing wall of crackling molten rock. It was imperative that something be done before the flow reached the harbour and made docking impossible. You have to stop for a moment to clear the mind of possible disaster and reflect on the advantages to living in this Titanic landscape. Summers of perpetual light, neighbours who don't overreact, a relaxing whiff of minerals . . . With his arms in the pool and his head turned towards the steaming hills, David says: 'Geothermal power, Mr Bond! An inexhaustible supply of energy, and very hot water. Tonight, we will be having lobster – of the human variety!'

★

For a sequence with so many startling images, it's odd that so few of the sonnets describe a visual scene. But in 143, a housewife puts down the baby at her breast and runs after a chicken. The baby cries. The housewife is the Dark Lady, the chicken the young man, and the baby William Shakespeare. The almost painterly farmyard predicament is well caught in the argument about wanting, chasing, and having-by-relinquishing. It has what I love most in poetry: lightness and lyrical complexity amid loss. 'So will I pray that thou mayst have thy Will, / If thou turn back and my loud crying still.' The fact he intends to pray should tell us something. Hope by its nature must always return, whereas those who leave seldom do.

★

Merri Creek's profile is dressed in green bunches and braids. Men with beards in shorts, with blue bulldog puppies; women wearing culottes, baggy T-shirts, backpacks, sunhats. Dogs leading their owners. Joggers ruining their knees and ankles. Cycling families, children asking, 'What was that snowman called?' 'Olaf.' 'I knew it was something beginning with O.' A mother to her overexcited son on his bike: 'Not everyone wants to hear your voice.' An angular, panting man running past wearing a singlet with 'MARBY

LIONS FC' on the front and 'Whatever It Takes' on the back. What is the origin of this contemporary malaise, the delusion that everything – life, one's dream – should be achievable? That all that's lacking to make wishes come true, to fulfil desire, is effort? Here comes effort. The little kid on stabilisers wailing unintelligibly, the father behind, glancing over at me and smiling and shaking his head while saying, 'Who wants a big chocolate milk? You're nearly there.' Wail, wail, wail. 'You don't want a chocolate milk?'

VII AVAST

The Presence at Drake Court

What's missing from this floor?
The furniture, but also the reason

it went, the argument
ripped out with the phone.

What's left – one dish of smear,
a sardine skeleton.

Don't bother asking the agent.
She has no opinion, in her kid coat

with her strangely burned fingers,
and so thin it may be she, too, eats

only by repute. Ask yourself, rather,
where is the flue for that rumour,

the one about a sister
and her brother's flight, his halt

in a dark-eyed European wood?
The sun's inventory reads: room.

The agent pales at the window,
fades into a forest of light

with no access to the particulars
for living off seeds, small kills,

alone in the out-there-somewhere
like a call-centre operative on Jupiter.

Barroco

If I were to write down a list
of everything I miss I'd miss
the most important thing,
an irregular pearl. Not gifts –
books on corvids, *Wild Lone*,
'Ballad of Gordon, Alpha Cock,
who clawed to death a fox
and Bedlington terrier' – or this

cod-oracle of signs, like Witch
the whippet's interpretable trot –
but the whole resolution
of a life by its own light: five
years nursing Flavio, who died;
endless sweeties, bad teeth;
your total inability to shout;
our lying in and our going out.

De Staël

The picture is a perch
and from the perch he's
drawn invisibly away.

From the moment he jumps
the window stays wide open,
the wind searches the land

for the wide, open moon
it mistakes for a lantern
and the trees and roofs

pine for still more shade.
They would like to be walls,
to fall straight and true.

The Voice

I get peculiarly involved
In things I do not want to do
And the matter's not resolved
Unless I speak to me as you.

Peculiarities revolved
About my head include the view
That we should be jointly dissolved,
That it would bring relief. Says who?

I'd like somehow to be consoled
By all the things we used to do.
The lack of them makes me feel old,
Peculiar, bodiless. It's true

I never want to be absolved
Of having been myself with you.
You're still peculiarly involved.
Fact of my life – and fancy, too.

Ever

On Albion Street the white roses are out
along with the bravely disappointed gardeners
in brown short-sleeve tops of durable stretch fabric
identifiable by the wash-label, if it exists.
The roses accept watering like automatons
with painful feelings not included in the booklet
and the wet tiles of the porch get stared at
by the husband whose wife behind the flyscreen
keeps a compound eye on his best efforts
with sprinkler and hose. What harm can he do?
Let's be kind. Let maintenance remain light
and the store of wisdom shut this afternoon,
drowsy as long marriage and the wait for the bell.
Because we're all waiting, our jaws shrinking
imperceptibly, the day tight under arms that hold
the idea of holding, if not the fact, dear.

Condensation

Drawn in steam was 'who', my first
   Stab at a word on the window.
It cried into a house on stilts,
Mid-stagger abode from *How & Why*.
   At the basement kitchen table

Among raised voices, waving hands,
   In our legless Diao Jiao Lou,
I sat back, wondering, not sure
If I'd made sense or spoiled for good
   The listening glass with kid babel.

Couple in the Rain

Are they OK, the Beresfords?
They test the cocoa outlines
of the yard's cobbles.
No, no. Nothing
is what they're looking for,
what the lost recipe required
or they'll admit they've lost.

This worm?
'That's not a worm.' This one?
'No, no. A worm is . . . well,
a worm is difficult to define.
I'll know one when I see it.' So,
it's *not*, thinks Mrs Beresford,
although it was.

To Mr Beresford's fine
mind (which gauges altitudes,
tip-speed and height-to-weight ratios)
she brings wifely patience,
inscrutable performances
of pert muddle,
because she's worried. Kind.

She wants to make him feel useful
and his incuriosity amuses her.
Only, sometimes, the sparing
gesture turns ticklish,
all down her back
in sliding drops
the size of a bird brain.

The Park Bench

'. . . oh dear, look at the mark . . .' – E. M. Forster

'What are you looking at?' says one, writing on the seat.
I'm looking – out of the corner of my eye – at the grey
    skin, blue trainers
and baseball cap, the tracksuit wrapped round kindling
    legs.
Or at the fake-fur trimmed parka over a cotton-print dress,
    and the head,
too small but enlarged by a kapok clock of hair. Or at the
    man with no teeth
who gets on the tram, sits opposite me and says, 'I had a
    good memory.
But I wouldn't want to go back to football. I'm going to
    try acting instead.

Didn't I tell you once before?' His gummy monologue
    takes in Abba,
working in the market, rubbish removal, gangs, New
    York, multiculturalism,
the death penalty (not death – capital punishment is death
    for others).
At the market where the toothless man worked, the lady
    with one leg who used to
sing light opera has been replaced by Blind Elvis, who does
    a passable 'Love Me Tender'.
At the old velodrome, a cyclist exercises his orbital
    greyhound.
I feel sorry for the poor creature. He is exhausted from
    running round the track

after his master and those revolving legs he's so attached to.

A whole tree in blossom looks like one elderflower.

Elm-suckers pop up far from the parent, sometimes around
     a tree

of a different species. It's as if they're hero-worshipping the
     Eucalypts,

who are cooler, but still kids. They've dropped branches,
     like scarves or hats,

in the spring gales. Elsewhere in the park: a dog being
     mobbed by magpies.

One black Labrador, quite frightened, led away by its owner.

People who can't praise others are children who were
     starved of love and possibly

underfed, and who now fear that when the pot next goes
     round

there will be nothing left in it for them. They have never
     recovered from the shock

of being introduced to the pot and its disappointments at a
     very early age.

A middle-aged man seeking a fresh start comes to Australia.

His visa allows him to work as he pleases. He makes contact
     with a younger man,

a trader and lawyer, who needs a valet. The power
     relationship is not obvious.

The confident younger man enjoys his financial dominance
     and prestige.

It becomes clear that he enjoys, too, a kind of sexual
     ownership

of his manservant, who enjoys it more, has an eye for his
     corner.

Then I went past an infants' school. It brought back strong memories

of St Stephen's, of a certain breathlessness in the face of the dining hall,

the long slope of hymn practice and the enormous minute playground

with its conical gradient leading to a drain. On the more level Australian terrain

in front of me white lines marked out an ignorable pitch. And on this pitch

were about fifteen six- or seven-year-olds and a bloke in a bush hat.

At 'Go', the kids ran up and down while their teacher sang 'The Simpsons'.

Lionel had a fall recently, went into hospital and will not be coming back,

so it has fallen to me to clear up the mess he left behind – a kitchen choked

with matter, boxes of rubbish, cartons of leftovers stacked on top of each other

hiding the fridge and stove, plastic bags full of unidentifiable white slop

hanging and dripping from the ceiling like dairy cultures. And isn't hoarding about faint possibilities, too? Hoarders are not attached

to the objects they hoard. They're attached to the possibility that a use will be found

for them. That the volume of crap they've accumulated will cover them, so to speak.

It's the low roller's only stake (all I have) in a game he can't win, and there's something heroic about it. Look, there will be a solution. Just look enough.

You Are Here. Bad Wolf. ('Oh, you bad, bad, bad, *bad* wolf!')

A Dying Fascist Misreads Plato

Nature is soul and often feverish with the longing to be
   used.

Since land desires to have a life, its self-justification is to be
   found
in souls who are capable of anger, who thirst and are
   immediately fulfilled
by the desire to be useful; not by the instinct for self-
   preservation.

Affections may assist the living, but place needs willing
   warriors.

They are in a class of their own, children, on the brow of
   the hill.
And the sweat on their faces is a sign of strength-in-
   abandon.
Go inside now, children; be glad of your fear; be still.

Death on the Ark

'Can't tell, Dad,' Shem says
every day for the first time, 'can't
tell if we're making *any* ground.'
The joke is quickly stowed, the snort
outraged the way some wives are
made to tolerate their husbands'
beards, though nothing about a fat
man's face grown ugly in the fork
of tropical lightning appeals.
'If there were a sign, a rock, a buoy,
a lull. If there were a star . . .'
Another strike portside, another fire,
mad dash with buckets, blankets, bells,
stampedes to nowhere once the smells –
woodsmoke and barbecue – drift lower.
'I like these crispy bits,' Shem's dad
says later, picking his teeth. 'The skin?'
'Species,' his son replies, whose memory fogs.
'Some kind of boiler-plate crustacean.'
But later still, alone, the patriarch retires
to mourn his favourite Sebright chick,
to pour out his distress upon
the coastless deep while Loris
hugs her branch, timidly
offering, perhaps encouraging.
The waters prevail. When shall they not?
Loris observes, chewing her smaller griefs.
There goes a leaf. There goes the dry season.

Noah's Owl

I won't see land again,
Only the face of these waters.
This is home now, this hollow trunk.
Crowded cypress. Uprooted tree:
No anchor to the world, a life that's wind.
Loose like the great cities sliding downhill
During the rains. A piece of global melt.
And hard sky, how you've changed!
You are tar, nails, planks, a barred light.
Heaven, prison.

According to my friend,
The wild boar, whose French is *trop correct*,
'Le soleil voilé se cache, tu vois, il est oublié.'
To which a pair of confined midwife toads
Respond as one, 'Reviens! Reviens!'

Robin

All orgies done, twice-
felled trees drop naked
in the wall-eyed streets.
A pregnant girl grapples
with laundry in the house
opposite. She's draping
sheets on drying racks and
rads, puffing her cheeks.
The sail of winter fills
a sky the colour of rice.
She's at sea when an arm
finds her in its harbour –
boyfriend, father-to-be.
My heart lifts, always,
with the orgiasts' bare
pines and toad-skinned
elder, and the varicose
rowan in whose hands
I raise, ounce-loud,
a song for cave days.

A Ship's Whistle

Years passed and I received no letter with the word 'trombone'.
  The distant cousins wrote, offered their shriller sympathies.
  'What's wrong with *us*?' Nothing I knew. Plugboard and isinglass,

grimoire and cwm, friends all. Still I felt horribly alone.
  Until one day it dropped through roundel-light onto the mat.
  I was tearing my dictionaries of hope – who, why, and what –

apart when it sounded, that note pressing for home. Trombone.
  And fearing it a dream was like waking in the wrong room,
  not daring to believe in your return, or having come

to my senses after sickness. Veneer, mirror and comb:
  objects that shivered as relief swelled under them, they drew
  lots to be turned to words which, soon as said, I knew

were brass. Years sliding past alone until – *avast!* – trombone.

VIII EXPERIENCE

Recollection imagines the might-have-been without interfering with the course of history. We hang upon the wall of memory, unable to advise or direct; content merely to observe the mental phantasms we are in the process of creating. We change a little, modify a scene, to suit our present sensitivities, though without feeling that what we are doing – imagining – is a physical as well as a mental act, an intervention made by some property of a person in actual history. Until, one day, someone who is not to be satisfied with merely looking inwardly, asks how the two things – the imagined past and the physical experience of the present – might be combined; how he might travel back in time, in what condition and armed with what knowledge. Such a person might be confined to an institution or made to take medication, or both at once. But in truth he poses no question that is not implicit in our understanding of the universe, and in the surprising yet well-established Einsteinian notion that, from the point of view of certain observers in the cosmos, travelling at certain speeds in certain trajectories, everything in our lives has already happened and none of us has been born yet.

ⒷB *editions*

Founded in 2007, CB editions publishes chiefly
short fiction and poetry. Writers published in
translation include Apollinaire, Andrzej Bursa,
Gert Hofmann, Agota Kristof and Francis Ponge.

Books can be ordered from www.cbeditions.com.